THE WORLD'S FASTEST

# Diesel

Published in December 2006

A catalogue record for this book is available from the British Library

ISBN 1 84425 420 8

Library of Congress catalog card no. 2006935939

Haynes Publishing, Sparkford, Yeovil,
Somerset BA22 7JJ, UK
Tel: +44 (0) 1963 442030
Fax: +44 (0) 1963 440001
E-mail: sales@haynes.co.uk
Website: www.haynes.co.uk

Haynes North America, Inc.,
861 Lawrence Drive, Newbury Park,
California 91320, USA

Printed and bound by J.H.Haynes & Co Ltd,
Sparkford, Yeovil, Somerset BA22 7JJ, UK

Designed by Lee Parsons and Richard Parsons

All images copyright LAT Photographic with the following exceptions:
David Tremayne Archive p18, 24, 39, 40, 41, 67, 135; Getty Images p74 (bottom), 75;
JCB p16, 42–47, 49; MPL p19, PRM Aviation Collection p25; Ricardo UK Ltd p31

# THE WORLD'S FASTEST

# Diesel

DAVID TREMAYNE

'It has been a very special few months. Being part of a team that built a record car, ran it in the UK, shipped it to Bonneville and set three records above 300mph (one Bonneville and two FIA), all in the space of three months.'

**Andy Green**

# CONTENTS

# FOREWORD

Growing up in Britain in the 1950s and '60s, it was impossible not to be enthused by the spirit of the land speed record-breakers. I read with awe about the exploits of men such as Stirling Moss, Phil Hill, Goldie Gardner and Donald Campbell as they pushed the limits of human endeavour. The names 'MG', 'Bluebird' and, of course, 'Bonneville', took on an iconic quality in my youthful mind.

It was a passion that was rekindled when we developed our own diesel engine. This was a landmark moment in the history of our company and one that encapsulated the best of British engineering. I was so impressed by our JCB444 engine that I dared to dream that it might form the basis of a record-breaking car. What better way could there be to demonstrate the strength of our engineering than to establish a new land speed record for a diesel car on the famous Bonneville Salt Flats?

It is impossible to thank everybody who contributed to the success of the JCB Dieselmax, but I feel I must single out a few team leaders without whom the attempt would not have happened and they are: Dr Tim Leverton, David Brown and Daniel Ward at JCB, John Piper at Visioneering, Matt Beasley at Ricardo, Ron Ayers and Simon Evans and David Hoyle at JCB Transmissions. Richard Noble – for all his help, advice and enthusiasm. And, of course, Andy Green, the fine car's driver.

I knew it was a bold challenge, and when I first made the suggestion I've no doubt that most people in the company thought I'd lost my marbles. But I had complete faith in JCB's engineering department. I knew that in Dr Tim Leverton we had an engineering director with the vision and the character to take on such a project, and in Dave Brown, project team manager, the remarkable commitment to get the job done. By the end of 2004 I was confident that we had the human tools needed to turn my crazy dream into a fantastic reality.

At this early stage I was also delighted to be able to call upon the services of Richard Noble OBE. Richard led the ThrustSSC team that achieved 763mph in 1997 and no one knows more about land speed record breaking, and what it takes to triumph against the odds. He suggested that instead of aiming just to break the existing record of 235.756mph we should target 300mph. I took a deep breath and agreed – the race was on.

Wing Commander Andy Green OBE is still 'the fastest man on earth' and epitomises the qualities that make the RAF the finest air force in the world. He is humble, dedicated, ferociously intelligent, immensely fit, hugely courageous and every inch a team player. I was honoured that he agreed to drive our car.

Ron Ayers is one of the finest and most forward-thinking aerodynamicists in the world, and he did an extraordinary job of shaping a JCB car that is not only highly efficient but beautiful too.

One of Andy's favourite expressions is that 'there is no "I" in team', and that sentiment best describes the spirit of the JCB Dieselmax team. It was a privilege to observe the coming together of such a talented group of people, that of course includes John Piper and his guys at Visioneering and all those at Ricardo. Each and every one of them worked endless hours to make the project a success and they should be immensely proud of their contribution.

In April we formally announced the project to the world's media and just four months later I travelled to Bonneville to witness our attempt on the record. Watching the JCB Dieselmax power across the desert at over 350mph was an emotional moment. It marked the realisation of my boyhood dream and it made me immensely proud, not just of the JCB team but also of the skills that have made British engineering the finest in the world.

I'm delighted to be able to introduce this book, which itself set new records for the speed at which it was written and published. David Tremayne is an award-winning writer and land speed historian whose beautifully written story is complemented by stunning photography to capture our contribution to the history of British land speed record breaking. I hope you enjoy it.

**Sir Anthony Bamford, Chairman, JCB**

Together with Andy Green and the victorious JCB Dieselmax: Sir Anthony Bamford and his family (left to right) Jo, Alice, Lady Carole and George, Bonneville Salt Flats, 23 August 2006.

# INTRODUCTION

I have to confess that when I first learned that a rumoured diesel car project involving Richard Noble and Andy Green was actually the brainchild of JCB, my heart sank. I had visions of British Leyland going land speed racing.

All I knew about the company then was that it built diggers, and its Chairman had some nice historic racing cars.

The first visit to the Rocester factory was an eye-opener, as was my first meeting with Dr Tim Leverton as we discussed the programme. Later I was touched on first meeting with Sir Anthony Bamford when he shook my hand and said, 'You're the chap who's helping us with this, aren't you?' I thought that was an elegant way of putting it.

Very soon it became clear just how serious the programme was. Several old friends from the motor racing world were engaged on it, together with other very serious players. All of them shared one thing in common: they were frighteningly clever. Nobody should underestimate just how smart they were.

What fascinated me most was that this was that rarest thing: a British land speed programme that had adequate funding from the start. That could have been spent foolishly or wisely because a full budget can be a double-edged sword, and it was a case of the latter. Being in the middle of a venture that was so well conceived and so well co-ordinated was impressive, and a whole lot of fun.

So was being a small part of a great enterprise that was such a significant showcase for British engineering. When I reluctantly tore myself away from one of my favourite places on earth and headed to Turkey for the Grand Prix, after Speed Week and the successful FIA record runs at Bonneville, I felt as if I'd received a blood transfusion. I've been fortunate to get close to several land speed record and Formula One teams, and hand on heart I can say that the JCB Dieselmax project was the slickest and most enjoyable of them all.

Its story was one of world class engineering, carried out by people who were world class, both professionally and personally.

To them all, as the French say, 'Chapeau'.

**David Tremayne**
Bonneville, Darlington and Tamagaki, 2006

'**Don't you dare mention Donald Campbell!**' Andy Green, as patient as ever under interrogation by the author.

**JCB Dieselmax: as sleek and slick as the team that ran it.**

**ACKNOWLEDGEMENTS**

My thanks for assistance in researching this book go to JCB Dieselmax team members Ron Ayers, Rod Benoist, Annie Berrisford, Colin Bond, Dave Brown, Mike Chapman, Chris Dee, Sophy Gardner, Teena Gade, Mark Guy, Brian Horner (especially for the model), Alastair Macqueen, Rob Millar, Richard Noble, Ian Penny, Duffy Sheardown, Allan Tolley and Daniel Ward; to the Fingal mob, especially Amanda Gadaselli, Peter Panarisi and Jules Tipler for comradeship (we'll always have the Econo Lodge!), Andy Ferraro and Brendan Prebo for memories of an amusing afternoon in Salt Lake City; to Mike Cook of Bonneville Nationals Inc (for his generosity) and Dave Petrali, the FIA's steward and a good friend from the Thrust days; and to 'Landspeed' Louise Noeth for her passion for land speed racing and showing me how to use a Wendover carwash.

Particular thanks go to team members Matt Beasley, Andy Green, John Piper and Tim Leverton for their help during the project, and subsequently for reading the manuscript and making helpful comments and changes that added to the story and prevented me from getting sideways and rolling end over end in print; and to Sir Anthony Bamford for writing the Foreword.

THE WORLD'S FASTEST DIESEL

# CHAPTER I
# WEDNESDAY, AUGUST 23

Mercifully, the sun had not risen as early as the JCB Dieselmax team on the morning of Wednesday, 23 August 2006.

Stand in its glare for too long on the Bonneville Salt Flats, 120 miles west of Utah's capital, Salt Lake City, and you risk the usual problem that catches out salt rookies: painful sunburn. And not just in the places you might expect; the light reflects off the crisp white salt, so you can be burned up the leg of your shorts, or even up your nostrils.

On the days when she visits Bonneville, that desolate lunar nothingness that is yet so hauntingly beautiful, Mother Nature delights in showing her crueller side whenever the chance presents itself. She is well versed in the art of inflicting pain, both physical and mental, upon men who go there in search of ultimates.

Andy Green was no stranger to her capricious whims, nor to the desire to venture into territory uncharted by other men.

Back when he was an RAF Squadron Leader, in 1994, his calmness under pressure and innate ability to get the best from his machines made him the stand-out choice as Richard Noble sought a driver for his nascent contender for supersonic speed on land: ThrustSSC. Three years later, on the Black Rock Desert in Nevada where Old Ma Nature played equally cruel tricks, as Noble would readily attest, Green faced the greatest challenge of his life as he piloted the big black jetcar through the sound barrier on his way to a world land speed record of 763.035mph. It still stands.

Almost a decade down the road, and now a Wing Commander, Green sat cocooned in the cockpit of the dramatic yellow and black JCB Dieselmax streamliner that had been born out of JCB Chairman Sir Anthony Bamford's desire to further the legacy of British achievement in the realm of record breaking. Ahead of him, Green had a two-stage turbocharged, 750bhp version of the humble JCB444 diesel engine that powered the company's familiar diggers; another was located behind his shoulders, giving the 30ft car 1,500bhp with which to achieve the goal of 350mph. No, this was no supersonic project, but putting all that power through four driven wheels, and seeking to increase the existing record for diesels by more than 100mph, presented a different kind of challenge that was no less worthy.

Twice already Green had claimed records from the hallowed salt; 317.021mph under SCTA-BNI timing during Bonneville's Speed Week the previous Friday, 328.767mph under FIA sanction the previous day. Each triumph had been received ecstatically by his team, the first with relief, the second with a measure of guarded expectation. Since the avowed goal had been to set a new record over 300mph and to give JCB the right to claim its car as the world's fastest diesel, that might perhaps have seemed sufficient. But goals are always fluid in motorsport, and the design speed had always, albeit privately, been 350mph. Now that was expected of him after a stunning first run of 365.779mph. It was now within his control alone either to deliver, or to make a mistake that would fritter away the speed that was in the bank from that remarkable first leg. All he had to do was repeat the performance on the mandatory return run, which had to be completed within an hour, and the job was done.

Green does not normally make mistakes. He is by nature a careful, disciplined man. When he was a pilot of Tornado fighters he had to be. The RAF has the highest expectations. But there had been an error, albeit a minor one, during the previous day's second run. Green had engaged the exhaust brake before he had cleared the measured mile, robbing Dieselmax of crucial speed. Green made light of it, but inside he was distraught. He is no control freak, but he doesn't like getting it wrong and he doesn't like letting his team down. So now, with the ultimate goal so close, he was determined that no such error should compromise their final achievement. If he had concerns about his tyres, which were rated by the team's own intensive empirical testing research to 350mph and were thus operating in marginal territory, they were secondary to his determination not to do anything to spoil this critical final run.

Calm as ever, he had watched his crew change all four wheels and tyres and ready the car for its journey to the south-western end of an 11-mile course. The salt was as good as it had been for the last 20 years, according to the experts who had been tasked

← **Hurtling north-east across the Bonneville Salt Flats, Andy Green had averaged 365.779mph as he sped through the measured mile in 9.842s on his first run on August 23, 2006. But his mandatory return pass, which followed this brief turnaround break, could not have got off to a worse start...**

THE WORLD'S FASTEST DIESEL

On the days when she visits Bonneville, that desolate
lunar nothingness that is yet so hauntingly beautiful,
Mother Nature delights in showing her crueller side
whenever the chance presents itself. She is well versed
in the art of inflicting pain, both physical and mental,
upon men who go there in search of ultimates.

↑ **Ricardo engineer Matt Beasley (left) supervises filling the ice tank prior to the final record run.**

↓ **Colin Bond in a JCB Fastrac prepares to push Green at the start of the first run. Push starts, a regular feature at Bonneville, save clutches and tyres.**

with its painstaking preparation. The car had proved five times now that it could exceed 300mph with insouciant ease. All of its myriad systems – the JCB engines developed by Ricardo, the chassis, suspension, steering and brakes designed and built by Visioneering – had now begun to work in harmony after a few false starts the previous week. The ultimate record, the final justification of the project, was there for the taking.

At 08.21 hrs that cool Utahan morning, Green felt the gentle bump which signalled to him that JCB Dieselmax had been pushed back into contact with the Fastrac tractor driven by Colin Bond. Within seconds Bond began to push him down the course until, at 40mph, he would brake the Fastrac and allow Green to freewheel initially and then select first gear prior to accelerating up to 3,800rpm and then start to run through the remaining gears as he gathered pace on the rush towards the measured mile that lay over the curved horizon.

Green knew the start sequence by heart: video on; rear engine start; front engine start. Check oil pressures, coolant pressures, other temperatures and pressures. Final check that parachutes and fire extinguishers are ready. Hinge back the safety cover for the driver's air switch. Select water injection on. Final check of all

switches and systems. Canopy shut. Rev the engines to 2,000rpm until the exhaust temperatures are above 200°C, then throttle back and thumbs up to engineer Alastair Macqueen. Receive 'Clear to Push' call from Macqueen. Feel nudge from Fastrac. At exactly 40mph, as Bond backs off, select first gear. Full power, accelerate to 1,800rpm (about 60mph), then start left foot braking, gradually increasing the brake pressure as the engines come on load. Wait to see 400°C exhaust temperatures for both engines, check the turbo boost is starting to climb (from 0.9 bar ambient to around 1.1 to 1.2 bar), then release brakes and wait for the boost to build. Maintain brisk acceleration to around 2,400, 2,500rpm (90mph) until the boost suddenly arrives in a rush. Drive one-handed at 100mph, selecting the coolant pumps separately as each engine comes on boost. Hands straight back to the steering wheel, just enough time to catch the rev limiter (3,800rpm). Second gear, steering and handling check, systems check on the right-hand screen to make sure all readings are in the green. Make small, quick corrections as the car scrabbles a little for grip as the tyres reach their friction limit. Back to the centre screen, 150mph, check the engines, then look out for the track's mile markers. 170mph, wait for the last change light (3,800rpm) before selecting third gear, another check of engines, systems, and handling, now over 200mph. Watch that the car may drift on salt ruts or in crosswind. More small, smooth corrections if necessary to hold it straight. Temperature in the engine cooling systems is now coming up to 90°C. 3,500rpm in fourth gear now, around 265mph, looking for anything over 350mph after change up to fifth gear at 3,700rpm...

As Green went through the now familiar process, selected first gear and Dieselmax began to head down the salt towards its date with destiny, the crew sprinted to their support vehicles and began to chase him to the far end of the track. But they had all gone a lot less than a mile when, as they accelerated over 100mph, an awful truth began to dawn on them.

In their puny road cars they were about to overtake the big yellow streamliner that should by now have been streaking away from them as it headed towards the point where the blue sky and the white salt met on distant the horizon...

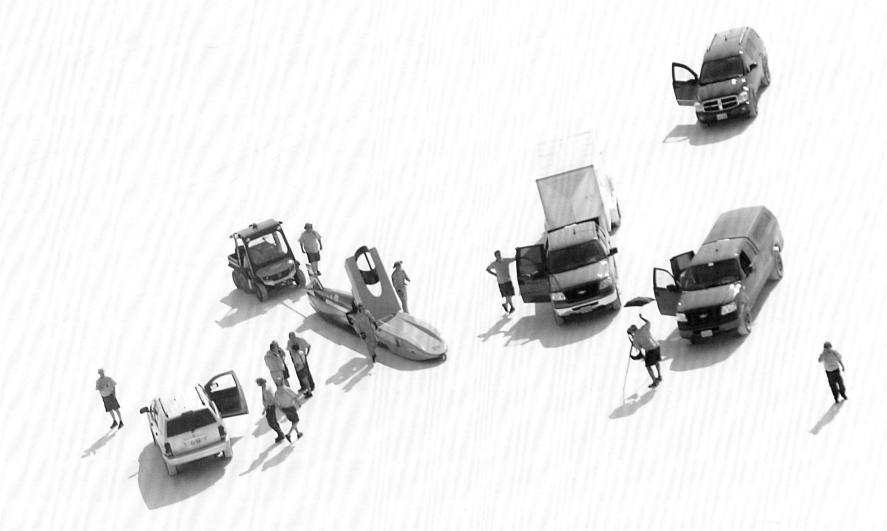

Remarkable aerial shot at the start of the record course underlines the puniness of mere mortals as they seek to outwit Mother Nature.

# CHAPTER 2

# THE CHAIRMAN'S DREAM

'It sounds silly, but...' Sir Anthony Bamford paused, looking a little sheepish, as he sat quietly in a corner beneath an awning in his team's pit, shielded from a broiling sun on the Bonneville Salt Flats, and considered the question why a company known the world over for manufacturing excavating equipment was mounting a challenge for a land speed record.

'The inspiration for JCB Dieselmax goes way back to being a schoolboy, reading *The Eagle* and *Boy's Own* in the late '50s,' he continued. 'And then more recently remembering that Stirling Moss got a land speed record back then with MG, to go with those set previously by Goldie Gardner and subsequently by Phil Hill. It was that type of thing, a little boyhood nostalgia. Remembering men such as Malcolm Campbell. And Richard Noble.

'The initial idea was mine, but it was reinforced very shortly afterwards by meeting Richard, who helped us a great deal with many, many aspects of the process. More than anything it was his enthusiasm, that is so infectious, that kept us going.'

Noble was one of an elite body of men who could lay claim to having once held a singular, romantic title: the Fastest Man on Earth.

Inspired himself by a chance sighting, as a six-year-old, of speedking John Cobb's Crusader jetboat, preparing for a water speed record attempt on Loch Ness in September 1952, Noble knew all about the power of dreams. That was why he was so well placed to understand Sir Anthony Bamford's.

When Noble decided to challenge American Gary Gabelich's 622.407mph land speed record, set with the Blue Flame at Bonneville on 23 October 1970, he immersed himself in a high-speed world of jet engines and hand-built streamlined cars; solid aluminium wheels and parachute braking systems; triumph and tragedy. A world in which the other greats of the game had names such as Henry O'Neal de Hane Segrave, Malcolm and Donald Campbell, George Eyston, Mickey Thompson, Craig Breedlove, Art Arfons, Bob Summers, Al Teague, and Don Vesco. These were the intrepid explorers who had ridden their streamlined chargers into uncharted territory in search of ultimate speed,

pushing the limits and raising the velocity. They went from 150 to 200mph, then 250 and 300, 350 and 400, and then, suddenly, after harnessing pure-thrust power in the '60s, through 500 onwards to 600mph.

Behind them, left in the shadows, there were other men, such as John Godfrey Parry Thomas, Lee Bible, Frank Lockhart, Athol Graham, Glenn Leasher, Noel Black and Nolan White. These were their fellow pioneers, men who had ventured out on the same trail but did not come back to tell their tales.

Land speed racing developed an appeal all of its own, for both participants and, particularly in the years between the two World Wars, expectant nations. Both Segrave and Malcolm Campbell received inter-war knighthoods for their daring deeds.

It was a chilling, cold-blooded game, devoid of the adrenaline rush of wheel-to-wheel competition. It was man against nature, and man against himself. 'If you're not a little bit afraid of this, you aren't playing with a full deck,' observed Breedlove, who would go on to break 400, 500 and 600mph and to survive one terrifying immersion in a brine lake after parachute failure at more than 500mph. Swimming ashore to greet his horrified crew, who naturally feared the worst after watching his Spirit of America career out of control down the Bonneville course, slice down a telegraph pole and then vault a dyke, he stood atop a bank, raised his fists to a sky that assuredly must suddenly have seemed bluer to him now than when he had started the run, and declared in a voice charged with the emotion of the moment: 'For my next trick... I'll set myself afire!'

In 1964 and '65 he and Arfons moved through nearby Wendover town like a pair of Western gunslingers, each knowing that the other would try to break whatever record they might set.

'I never sleep the night before I drive,' Arfons confessed. 'You think about everything that might happen. But I worry most about the other man inside me and what he'll do when he gets into the car, because I know that at that point fear and caution leave him.

'It's the other me, climbing into that car; they tell me I'm white

Sir Anthony Bamford, industrialist and patriot, was inspired to emulate the heroic deeds of men such as Sir Malcolm Campbell and Stirling Moss in the realm of record-breaking.

**↑ Campbell, in his famous Bluebird, was the first man to break the world land speed record on the Bonneville Salt Flats. On September 3, 1935, he achieved his last avowed goal with the machine by setting a new record of 301.129mph, and ushered in a new era.**

as a ghost. Then the motor starts and it's a Jekyll and Hyde thing. The power becomes music to me and I'm in another world. Only after that does the fear crawl in again, like fog, telling me what a fool the other man has been.

'When I'm at Bonneville I can't wait to get away. But once I'm away, I can't wait to get back.'

Noble's own turn for death or glory came, not at Bonneville after all, but on Nevada's Black Rock Desert on 4 October 1983 when he drove his Thrust2 jetcar to 633.468mph, finally erasing Gabelich's mark after a bruising nine-year struggle. That record in turn fell to fellow Englishman Andy Green at 714.144mph on 25 September 1997, in the ThrustSSC supersonic contender that Noble had masterminded. On 15 October that year Green smashed through the sound barrier on land with 763.035mph, a record that has never been challenged.

The pure-thrust cars quickly outstripped their wheel-driven brethren once the jet engine became the powerplant of choice, but there were other honourable efforts in the latter category: in October 1965 Bob Summers broke Donald Campbell's hard-won 403.1mph wheel-driven record with 409.277mph in his glorious

Goldenrod; in August 1991 Al Teague shaded that with 409.786mph; in October 2001 the great Don Vesco raised that to 458.455mph.

In smaller categories, men such as Gardner, Moss and Hill set class records over 200mph for MG, their stories equally heroic, their challenges equally taxing.

This, then, was the rich tapestry that shaped Bamford's thoughts as he watched his company's first diesel engine undergoing trials on the dynamometer at the Ricardo factory in Shoreham-on-Sea.

'It has always been a family tradition that the way to make progress is to push forward and to seek new challenges,' he explained. 'I was advised by many people that building our own engine would be a mistake, yet we have proved our critics wrong. The JCB444 has been acknowledged as a remarkable piece of engineering, and I believed that the engineering programme to build the world's fastest diesel-powered automobile was precisely the sort of challenge that we should welcome and accept.

'Ricardo was doing quite a lot of work and we had a big team down there. And one day I asked one of the people, just out of curiosity, what the diesel world land speed record was. And they looked it up in their archives and it was 235mph. And I thought, "Well, you never know. As a way of showcasing our engine business, it might be the thing." But I put it to the back of my mind, because we hadn't even produced the engine then.'

Ian Penny, global director of diesel engineering at Ricardo, a firm of consulting engineers, was present that day and said: 'I think ever since Sir Anthony saw the first 444 engine run, he had wanted to go and break records with it. There were loose discussions going on for a long time, different concepts that migrated over time into a streamliner.'

'Once we were about to start production in 2004 I suggested the idea to Dr Tim Leverton, our group engineering director,' Bamford continued, 'and he said, 'Well, we need to get this thing going fully in production first, then we'll look at it.'

'Our family has always had a passion for engineering, a passion for manufacturing in Britain, and a passion for trying to succeed. I just thought, "Why shouldn't Britain do things like this?" You know there are other examples where Britain succeeds in engineering, and has been doing so for years, and we aimed to continue doing that. The idea was just part of that.

'Richard came to see us early on through a mutual friend, and he is an inspiring fellow if you can just damp him down a bit! You know what I mean! He's great, and he told us so many short cuts and gave it his blessing and introduced us to Andy Green. It went on from there.'

One of the fascinations of the JCB Dieselmax project was that it was that rarest of animals: a record project that was fully funded from the start. Normally, these things begin with one man's dream and he then clambers on to the treadmill of seeking the funding to get the job done. That was what Noble had to do with both his Thrust2 and ThrustSSC programmes, both of which came perilously close to failure on countless occasions due to financial shortfalls. But here was something for which the funding existed, turning the whole thing the other way around.

'I do admire what Richard was doing, because he was trying to put his thing together, running and driving it, getting the sponsors, sorting the engineering,' Bamford admitted. 'It has been a lot easier for us because we haven't gone for sponsors. The sponsors that we have are all people who have been involved in the project, such as Ricardo, Corus and UGS.

'The only sponsor I sought was BP. I wrote a letter to Lord Browne there, thinking that they would like to be associated. After all, BP and Castrol were the people who were always with British land speed record attempts. And I thought they would want to be involved. But they didn't want to do it.'

It isn't difficult to envisage a television advertisement, where Mondeo man is refuelling his car as Andy Green suddenly pulls up alongside him in JCB Dieselmax. The outrageous juxtaposition of the near 30ft long yellow streamliner stopped at the fuel pumps.

'What are you doing here?' incredulous Mondeo man asks.

'Well, I use the same diesel fuel you do,' Green replies...

It should have been a marketeer's dream, like the big brown UPS truck and the US advertisements that reflect that company's high-level involvement in NASCAR racing.

'They didn't want to know, and strangely didn't seem to want to promote diesel at all,' Bamford revealed. 'I just thought it was disappointing. I would have liked to have had BP's flower on the side, I think it would have gone well with it, or Castrol's logo. Maybe I'm a bit silly and nostalgic about it. I remember things like that, Malcolm Campbell, KLG spark plugs. But honestly, we didn't try hard enough because we didn't have time, and this has been the luxury we've had doing it on our own, not touting ourselves around. It's all yellow, it's all JCB.'

Perhaps because of that, JCB Dieselmax would become one of those icons that captured the public's imagination.

**Stirling Moss and the MG EX181 at Bonneville on August 23, 1957, where he set international class records ranging from 224.70 to 245.64mph. Forty nine years later, to the day...**

# CHAPTER 3
# GETTING SERIOUS

**D**r Tim Leverton always tells the story of his initial involvement in the JCB Dieselmax project with a big smile and a rueful shake of his head.

He had joined JCB in April 2003, as director of group engineering with board responsibility for JCB power systems. His remit was twofold: to upgrade systems and infrastructure and to bring the engineering group into line with the growth there had been in the previous period; and to take responsibility for putting the new JCB444 diesel engine into production. The company had never ventured into such territory before, and critics regarded the step as beyond its core competence. The £80 million development cost and the bespoke Dove Valley Park manufacturing facility marked the biggest single investment made by the company in its 60-year history. The five-year design and development process had included more than 100,000 hours of testing.

Initially the engine was targeted at JCB's two key mid-range products: the backhoe and the telescopic handler. It was thus absolutely essential that it was delivered in time.

Leverton therefore had a high level of responsibility and was the obvious confidante when Sir Anthony Bamford felt it was time to share his dream of setting a speed record with the new powerplant. But the engineer, who already felt that he and the company had more important and immediate things to address, readily admitted that he was nothing like as enthusiastic about the idea.

'I'd been here six months when one day the Chairman said to me, "We'd like to do something special with the engine," and mentioned the land speed record. I'd been here long enough to understand that such unusual things did arise from time to time. I just smiled at him but said in my mind, "You're crazy!"

'We did some background work to look at what that would mean but it wasn't at a high level. We just got our heads down and carried on with the engine production programme.

'The subject came up again in 2004 and by this time the Chairman had got it into his head that the right way to approach it would be with a Le Mans car, and to put our engine into that. He

said to me, "You worked with Audi. Get one of their Le Mans cars and we'll do a record." We hadn't put that much thought into the vehicle side of it before. We'd actually talked about using an Ultima kitcar, and established that the engine would actually fit into that vehicle. But it was immediately obvious to me that a Le Mans car was totally unsuitable as a vehicle for this, like any race car which is downforce-oriented is unsuited to high-speed straightline racing. To be honest, I thought he'd just forget about it. So again I didn't give much thought to it, but it kept coming up at regular periods and the Chairman sent me some press clippings of an electric land speed car. He read a lot of technical magazines.

'As we went through 2004, I realised that it was becoming more serious. Then I think he'd had a conversation with Willie Green, who raced his historic cars, and Willie had told him we'd need to do something very different. So one day, in September that year, the inevitable happened and I bumped into Anthony face-to-face on the executive staircase at JCB World Headquarters in Rocester. And he put his finger on my chest and said, "I want you to take this seriously. I want you to do something about this project!"

'This time I said, "Yes, Boss!"'

Bamford remembered: 'I think Tim had just kept a file on it, until I said I really wanted to do something. Then he did get going. I would think there had been a six-month lull since I'd first mentioned it. The search for the next innovative step, new materials and methods of production, is a cornerstone of our business, allied to a very strong sense of corporate adventure. This just seemed perfect to me.

'Tim brought on board some very good people, some of our people, such as David Brown, who have done a sterling job. Then came Ricardo and eventually Visioneering. They were all excellent people who were all pulled together by the team leader.'

Bamford told Leverton that he had invited Richard Noble up to Rocester to talk about land speed racing. 'He said: "You can take him through all the work you've done on this,"' Leverton recalled. 'We all thought, "Oh, goodie..." Well, that week before Richard

↑ **Tim Leverton: a gifted and passionate automotive engineer and the mastermind behind the JCB Dieselmax project. He would catch a serious dose of salt fever before it was over.**

◄ **Matt Beasley gives Sir Anthony Bamford a rundown of the process by which the specific power output of his engine had been multiplied by a factor of five.**

↑ **One of the initial**
**considerations was to use**
**Audi's 2004 Le Mans R8 race**
**car powered with a single**
**JCB444 engine.**

arrived more work got done on the programme than in the whole previous three months!'

Leverton had been thinking that they might hit 250mph with 750bhp. 'In the background things had moved on quite a lot and by that stage we were on the verge of going into production with the standard 444 engine and a lot of the uncertainties with it were resolved. So at that point we began to work on some serious calculations in terms of what it could ultimately develop. We fairly quickly felt that something around 700–750bhp was thinkable using a combination of parameters that we were aware of from engine research, in terms of things like cylinder pressures. The structure of the engine could withstand very high boost, and we planned to use two-stage turbocharging.

'But when Richard came up to Rocester at the beginning of December 2004 the first thing that he said to us really got us focussed: "Well, you've got to go through 300mph." He started talking about two engines. So metaphorically that screwed up

everything we'd done on the vehicle since the start! He asked us what we could do with the engine, and a lot of other questions, and within an hour and a half we'd come up with the idea of two engines and 1,500bhp. It wasn't a Eureka moment; just pure mathematics. If you want a car to go 300, 350mph, you want that sort of power.

'Richard gave us an invaluable insight into the land speed record. If you want to build a wheel-driven streamliner in America, you go on the Internet and you can buy an 1,100bhp engine for around £7,000. A lot of the concentration is on the car rather than the engine. Our original concept was built entirely around the engine.

'We talked about a variety of things, John Cobb's Railton Special, all that sort of thing, and as we got to know Richard we were all really impressed by his enthusiasm and his knowledge, and his humility, to be honest. We didn't know quite what to expect, but he was such a charming character that we were all won over immediately with the whole idea. We'd already started sketching that first morning...

'Once we had sat down with Richard, I was convinced we could do it and that we would be successful. He talked about Carl Heap's diesel truck and Roy Lewis' diesel-powered Chassis Engineering Special, and it was clear that he was talking about something very different to what we'd been talking about. He talked about people such as Cobb, and that night when I got home I totally believed that we could break the diesel land speed record with our engine. The effect that Richard had was to inspire us.

'When I reported back to Sir Anthony, he smiled and said, "Okay, now go and sort out how we can do it."'

The next stage was to meet again with Noble, at Millennium Point in Birmingham. 'That really was an inspirational place to start. We scoped out a three-phase programme. We started with a desktop study starting in the first quarter of 2005; then we'd aim to prove our concept of what we were doing by the middle of the year; and then we'd make a decision on whether to go ahead in September, after we'd visited Bonneville Speed Week in August.

'In hindsight, maybe we should have kicked off a bit sooner, because the information we had by July was the same as what we still had by September. So we could have gone a bit earlier in terms of getting the design started, but pretty well we stayed in that mindset.

'The Railton Special was on display at Millennium Point. It was still in its original condition, quite remarkable, never been touched or overhauled. It had this special patina. The bodyshell was raised on stilts so you could see the machinery, the S-shaped chassis with two Napier Lion engines mounted in the places where the chassis curved, and four-wheel drive. At first, all you see is pipes and bits everywhere, and you need to take a couple of hours to assimilate what it is. It helps if you have a cutaway picture to help you understand how its main chassis works and how they got everything in and solved each of the problems of installing those big Napier Arrow 12s. We pored all over it and admired what it represented in terms of engineering elegance. It's a beautiful, remarkable piece of work. So elegant.

'Richard wanted to sit in the cockpit, but the guy on duty wasn't so sure. Richard said, "Well I am a British land speed record holder." A bit of a crowd had gathered, and it went from there. I had my photo taken sitting in the cockpit, too! For me, seeing the Railton was a source of what could be possible.' Noble sowed the seed that in 50 years' time, JCB's streamliner might similarly inspire engineers of the future.

Leverton promised Bamford a written proposal before Christmas. 'On Christmas Eve 2004, a Friday, I faxed it to him in Barbados, or wherever he was. My conscience was thus clear.

'I was sitting chatting with my secretary about old Mr Bamford, Joe, who would give people a job at lunchtime and want them to report back to him by four o'clock. It was 1.45pm, and at Christmas Sir Anthony would habitually announce at two o'clock that we could go home early. We were making jokes, ready to run to our cars, when the phone rang. My secretary said it was Sir Anthony. I said, "Yeah, right." But it really was him. He'd received my fax, and he just said, "Do it." So suddenly, we were on.'

Leverton's background in engineering encompassed his spell at BMW, where he was chief engineer on the Rolls-Royce Phantom. Then he had supervised production of the JCB444 engine. 'At that time the company had a patchy reputation for bringing a new product to market. It had made this massive investment and one of the reasons why I was hired was to steward that project. Now it wasn't my engine, I'm not an engine guy. My job was to ensure that the bet Anthony had made on the engine wasn't going to cost us the company, because it was going to be installed in all our core products. And we did it very well, and I had a lot of similar feelings with our team there, Alan Tolley and the guys who were actually making the engine, that I would later have with the Dieselmax team. And that intensity remained until we launched the engine in the first few months. So that was my intermediate step with the company, if you like.

'Then I started out on the land speed project almost with, "How on earth do I handle Anthony with this?" Because he wants to do this, but do I believe him? Is it just a flippant thing? And then I realised that it wasn't flippant at all and we started talking about it. He said it had been a dream and, as it happened, by the time we had got to Bonneville everyone in the team had appropriated the dream for themselves and thereby fulfilled themselves at the same time as realising it for Sir Anthony. And for him to do that, and to act in the

**Richard Noble: the former land speed record holder and creator of the supersonic ThrustSSC provided crucial guidance to the project in its formative stages.**

John Cobb's 400mph Railton Special, exhibited at Millennium Point in Birmingham, proved an inspirational mechanical masterpiece as JCB's team of engineers began to formulate their own record car concept.

way that he did, which was to be very supportive but not interfering, was a tremendously generous thing. You could have said because it was a hobby thing of his that he might have put his fingers into it every week, which would have been okay, but he didn't do that.'

They needed a codename for the project, which was to be kept so secret that for 15 months only half a dozen people within the company had the faintest idea of its existence.

'Sir Anthony kept referring to it as our land speed record project, and that wasn't quite as secure as I wanted!' Leverton said with a rueful laugh. 'I saw the movie *The Aviator* in the cinema around that time, and there was an elegant bit where Howard Hughes went for the air speed record with his Hughes H1 aircraft. He succeeded, too, but ran out of fuel and crash-landed in a cabbage field. But his record was 352mph. Anyway, I decided to call the project H1. I even changed my laptop password to a new six-letter code: lsr350.'

JCB had two major assets when it started the H1 project programme: the enthusiasm of its Chairman and the financial wherewithal. But the company itself had zero background in any sort of sporting endeavour, apart from Sir Anthony's collection of historic racing cars. However, its third asset was a very strong core

engineering competence via men such as Leverton, which would prove crucial in making up ground in a hurry.

In January 2005 there was a Project Kick-Off Meeting at Millennium Point in Birmingham, which featured Leverton, Noble, senior JCB engineers Alan Tolley (the engines director) and Simon Evans (the chief of transmissions), and Ian Penny, the global director of diesel engineering from Ricardo. Noble had also brought in Ron Ayers, the former Bloodhound missile designer whose quiet-spoken genius had unravelled the secrets of supersonic speed on land while he was investigating the aerodynamics for Noble's ThrustSSC record breaker.

'We could show everyone the Railton,' Leverton explained. 'Richard did a very good job during that day of grounding us in terms of just what we were tackling, and how we should approach it, and we agreed some fundamental ground rules in terms of how the project should be operated.'

Immediately, even on that first day, they established a 'default to safety' decision-making process. Right from the word go everything had to be safe before they made the next step; to ensure this, the project didn't just automatically default to making the next step,

going to have?' Penny said. 'What is the car going to look like? Where are the engines going to go? Where is the driver going to go? All that sort of stuff.

'We then went through various milestones of defining the concept and then validating it. We invested a lot initially and got to the point of a car that looks like it does today. Then a specification went out to various people, including an engineering company in Coventry called Visioneering. I think they were always going to be involved to some extent because they were going to do the bodywork, but they would also tender for the build contract.

'Once we got to that stage it was outside of our core business. We are not really into making one-off race vehicles and carbon fibre bodywork. So at that stage we handed the project back to JCB while carrying on exclusively developing the engine.'

Leverton had approached Clive Hickman of Ricardo and invited him to partner JCB instead of simply being a supplier. Ricardo's work on the JCB444 engine up to 2000 made it a natural choice.

**The film 'The Aviator', and Howard Hughes' 352mph Hughes H1 racer, gave Leverton the inspiration for the codename he adopted: Project H1.**

unless all safety aspects had been fully considered and satisfied. 'That was really necessary,' Leverton conceded, 'because you can get carried away in the excitement.'

'That meeting was when the project really began,' Penny recalled. 'Typical Richard, he had an old newsreel film of the land speed record with all the crashes, the culture and the history. He explained that you put yourself on the line, personal and corporate reputations, showed us all the things that had gone wrong, and outlined the culture of how you do it properly.'

Leverton created a core steering team after the kick-off meeting, which met every fortnight through the first half of 2005 and drove the concept process. Noble and Ayers were key members, and Dave Brown joined in April. While Penny nominated Matt Beasley, one of Ricardo's best people from advanced engineering and special projects, to lead the project technically at this stage, and effectively to do the heavy lifting, the steering group debated and thought through the decisions which determined the path through the concept development.

'Through 2005 we went through an evolutionary stage of saying exactly how much power do we need, how many engines are we

↑ **Driver Andy Green, chief designer John Piper and project mentor Richard Noble (foreground), at the presentation of the project to Sir Anthony Bamford at Rocester in 2005.**

'Because of our other workload we didn't have the capacity to allocate a team from engines because the 444 had only gone into production on 1 November,' Leverton explained.

'We started work on specifying the engine in detail, and tried to understand the issues we would face in conceiving the vehicle. Within months we had established the general arrangement of the car, and throughout the process we became more and more confident that it was right. Having approached Andy Green about being the driver in March 2005, we were then able to incorporate his input. Then we started to think about who was going to be our partner in terms of car design and build.'

He also formalised the aims of the project and put them into their definitive form around this time.

'On the face of it we are the last people to be going after land speed records, but actually there is a very practical purpose to this project. Our intention is to prove and publicise the quality and performance of the JCB444 engine on the world stage. In doing this we have already begun to learn valuable engineering lessons that have a direct application to future iterations of the unit, which means that our customers will benefit.

'The programme is also a perfect demonstration of the engineering talent within the company, and of its forward-thinking and aggressive philosophy.'

Much later, he would confess: 'I thought we'd run the programme like any other corporate project: take all the risks out, test it, and get on with it...'

Little did anyone at that stage know that Project H1 would follow its own distinctive, and very different, path. Or that it would be far from smooth.

Three of the prime movers behind the success of JCB Dieselmax: John Piper, Sir Anthony Bamford and Tim Leverton.

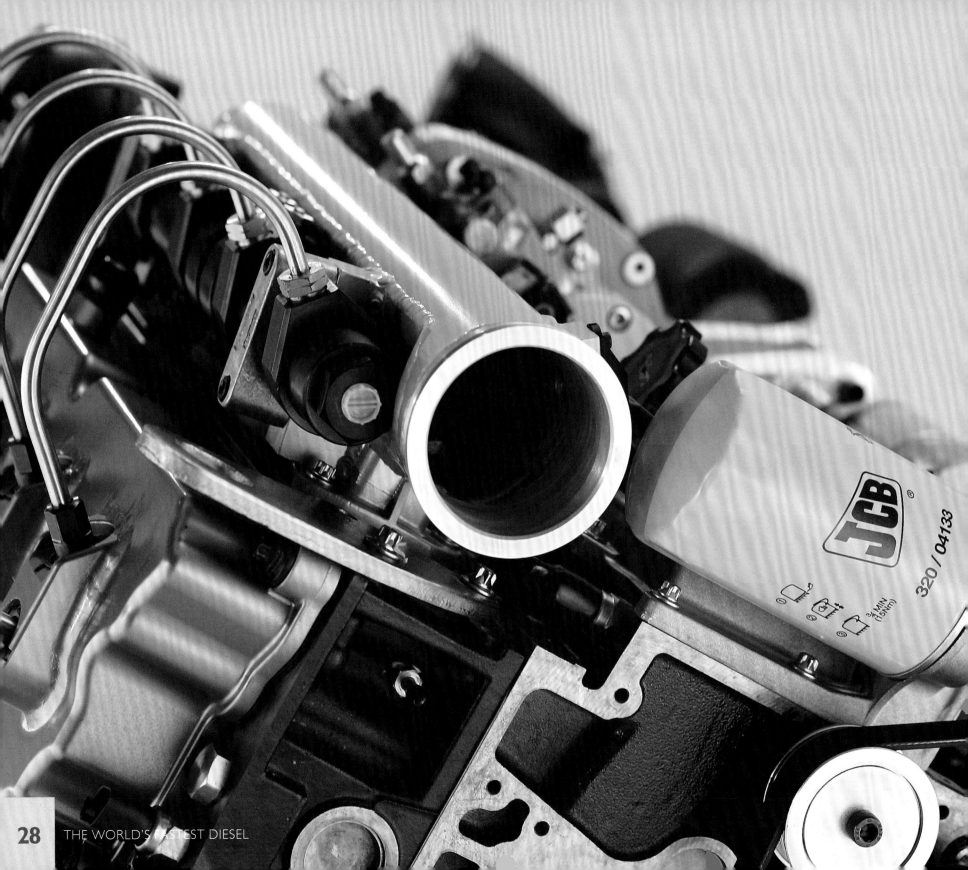

# CHAPTER 4

# THE HEART OF THE PROJECT

Project H1 always had that one very clear directive: the JCB444 diesel engine from the lowly backhoe digger was to be the heart of the Bonneville streamliner.

How a humble 140bhp engine was thus developed into a 750bhp racing unit, and how its specific power output was multiplied by a factor of five without adverse effect on its reliability, is one of the most triumphant stories in 21st-century British engineering history.

The JCB444 met four key design targets: strong construction; high torque at low engine speeds; reduced noise levels; and future-proofing for the next steps in emissions legislation. Also in its favour were a very strong crankshaft, an exceptionally stiff cylinder block structure, and a substantial cast-iron bedplate that closed the bottom of the engine.

It was a four-cylinder inline diesel with four valves per cylinder and 1.1 litres per cylinder. Hence the 444 nomenclature which reflected the 4,400cc displacement achieved via a bore and stroke of 103x132mm. Various power outputs were available, from 74bhp naturally aspirated up to 100bhp turbocharged and 140bhp charge-cooled turbocharged. Peak torque, achieved at only 1,300rpm, was 320Nm, 425Nm and 525Nm respectively. Multi valve technology and centrally positioned fuel injectors guaranteed combustion efficiency and therefore economy. At the time it was the only engine of its kind designed specifically for its intended application.

Sir Anthony Bamford's dream to use it in a land speed record vehicle would certainly prove its versatility and validate its inherent excellence, but in a totally different – and extremely demanding – engineering environment. And, as Leverton dictated, 'I wanted it to be the standard design block and have exactly the same fundamental architecture. It had to be recognisably the JCB444 engine. And we ended up with a stock block, with only internal tweaks, cylinder head and bedplate.'

Some of the parameters that made the engine such a strong industrial powerplant militated against its use as a racing engine, however, and created serious development challenges, as Ian Penny explained.

'The engine was designed to go into a digger. Diggers have scoops at the back, and on a backhoe loader you don't want the front to tip up when your bucket is full. So it wasn't ever designed for light weight. If anything it was designed up to a weight target, about 470kg in standard trim. To put that into context the Judd racing engine with similar capacity and power weighs 150kg for 670bhp.

'The stroke is 132mm compared to the Judd's 72, the standard operating speed is around 2,200rpm, and one of its pistons, for example, weighs 2.3kg, or four times the weight of a typical passenger car's.

'So if you wanted to break a speed record, you wouldn't start from here!

'Ideally you want power and light weight because otherwise you've got all that inertia to accelerate. Typically, to get a lot of power you want lots of cylinders. If you look at the Audi and Peugeot Le Mans engines, for example, they were V12s. That's because in a diesel engine with common rail fuel injection, the number of cylinders or the number of injectors governs how much fuel you can put in. In our case we've got four injectors, making 750bhp. The Audi has 12 injectors making 650bhp, so do the maths and our injectors are doing about four times as much work as those in classic racing engines. And that is a huge challenge, just to get that amount of fluid through the injector.'

The first step in increasing power output was relatively straightforward. The engine was bored and stroked to 5 litres. The greatest challenge lay in getting sufficient air and fuel into it to increase its power, and then managing that air and fuel flow and the associated heat generated by two-stage turbocharging operating at over 6 bar.

Ricardo considered several types of boosting system. 'We looked at single-stage and two-stage turbocharging, and then hyperbar, which was the most off-the-wall,' project director Matt Beasley revealed. Hyperbar runs almost independently of the

← **Although it was installed at 10 degrees from the horizontal, the JCB444-LSR engine shared the same cylinder block, head and bedplate as its humble brethren from the company's range of diggers.**

Power was transmitted via a JCB-designed stepper gearbox, an Xtrac transaxle and a multi-plate clutch.

With an operating pressure of 1,600bar, precision tolerances, alignment and careful assembly were essential to prevent potentially dangerous fuel leaks.

engine, having an additional fuel burner in between the turbos, so you can keep them operating at their optimum condition. A conventional turbocharger only takes the exhaust energy from the engine; hyperbar effectively feeds it another energy supply.

'It gives you the potential for a lot more boost,' Beasley said, 'but we didn't go that way because it takes a lot of focus away from the engine. We wanted to do this with technology, and an approach, which was relevant to the real world. That's why we chose two-stage turbocharging. Almost everything you could see on the JCB444-LSR engine will appear on diesel engines in the near future.'

Ricardo calculated that for the speed record attempt, the two engines would require an intake airflow of almost five tonnes per hour. Moreover, this would need to be delivered at the 4,290ft altitude of the Bonneville salt flats, where ambient air pressure is 85 per cent of that at sea level. While the production engine required a boost pressure of 1 bar, the two engines installed in JCB Dieselmax required over 6 bar absolute at full power. The scale of this challenge can be appreciated in comparison with around 3 bar absolute for a diesel Le Mans racer, and around 4 bar for the turbo-era Formula One cars of the '80s.

In meeting this significant air handling challenge, Ricardo developed a two-stage turbocharger system with both inter-stage and after-cooling, in order to deliver the required airflow across the engine speed range. A water injection system provided a further level of charge cooling to protect the pistons and valves in what was an ultimate test of durability.

The fuel system was equally challenging. 'Getting the fuel and air in was the single most difficult thing as far as I was concerned,' Beasley said. 'The fuel system was a big challenge, getting the engine to run the speed we needed to achieve the power we needed.'

The system was entirely bespoke for the JCB444-LSR application. 'Every bit of it was unique,' Penny explained. 'To move that amount of fuel under 1,600 bar pressure, and to keep it reliably sealed, was a significant challenge.'

Ricardo had excellent combustion system expertise, from its experience working on race diesels with John Judd, and on other

projects. If the engine was the heart of the vehicle, then the combustion system was very much the heart of the engine, and the JCB444-LSR engines used Ricardo's High Speed Diesel Race (HSDR) direct injection combustion technology. Fuel was delivered via two parallel high pressure pumps to a common rail system delivering an injection pressure of 1,600 bar. The cylinder head had to be modified slightly to encompass the larger injectors required for the HSDR system, and the actuation time for each injector was very subtly different once they had been tuned individually to their respective cylinders.

Demonstrating the robust design of the original JCB444 engine, the valve train was carried over substantially in its original form with the exception of high temperature specification exhaust valve material and uprated springs.

Hand-in-glove with the revised induction and fuel systems, a completely redesigned piston was used with a large, quiescent combustion chamber with reduced overall compression ratio, and specific features to reduce the risk of thermal damage to the combustion chamber components. Adequate piston cooling was assured by doubling the size of the original oil cooling jets in addition to the provision of supplementary jets, which together increased the cooling oil flow for each piston by around 600 per cent. A completely new, fully machined connecting rod was also incorporated, including a significantly enlarged small-end bearing to increase strength and robustness. While giving a longer stroke, the billet-machined crankshaft was lightened but retained its main and big end bearing sizes and shells.

Weight-saving measures were also vital. They took out any material in the cylinder block that was redundant, such as bosses for power take-offs and various brackets; and the gearcase and bell-housing were replaced with bespoke aluminium components. Besides the crankshaft, the camshaft was also lightened, as were gears. The JCB444-LSR engines were 20 per cent lighter as a result, weighing in at around 375kg.

The results of Ricardo's engine development were highly impressive. Peak power rose to 750bhp at 3,800rpm (almost twice the standard 444's rotational speed) and peak torque to 1,500Nm. The JCB444-LSR engine therefore generated more

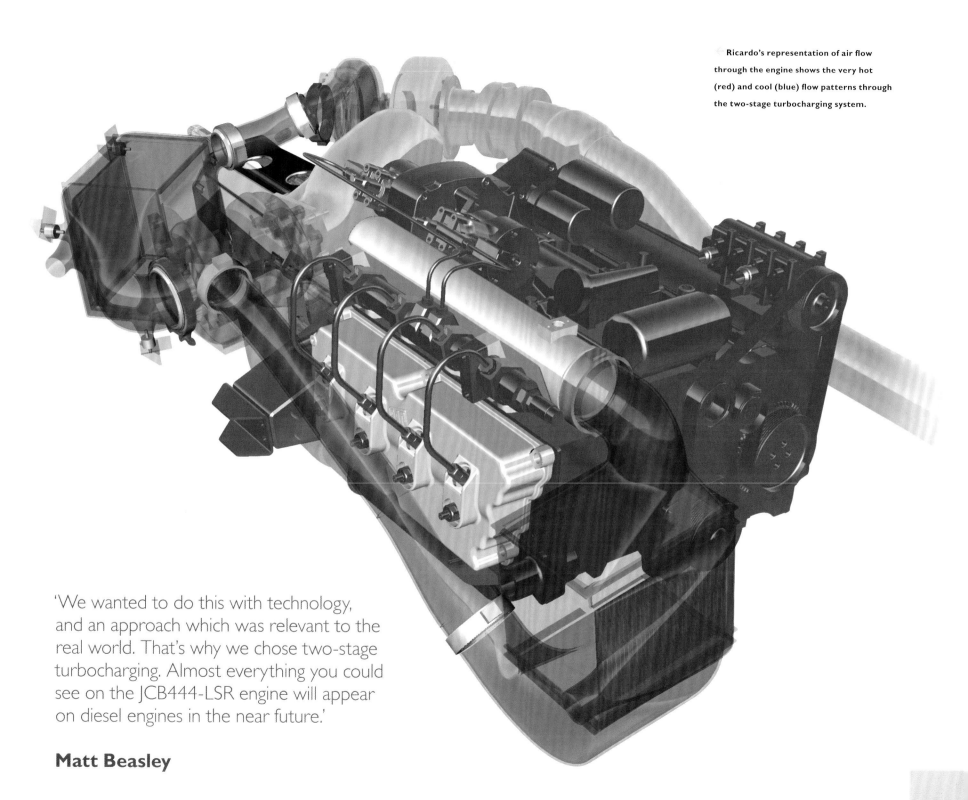

'We wanted to do this with technology, and an approach which was relevant to the real world. That's why we chose two-stage turbocharging. Almost everything you could see on the JCB444-LSR engine will appear on diesel engines in the near future.'

**Matt Beasley**

'We are fully confident that it is easily going to be the most efficient land speed record car there's ever been. It is probably more fuel efficient running at motorway speeds than most passenger cars. Compared to a Formula One car it is three or four times the weight, twice the power and probably half the fuel consumption at 50 per cent higher speed.'

**Ian Penny**

With five times the power of the standard engine – 750bhp and 1500Nm of torque – the JCB444-LSR unit's 150bhp/ litre exceeded all other motorsports applications and made it the world's highest specific power diesel car engine.

than five times the power of the production version and, at 150bhp/litre, exceeded even motorsports applications as the world's highest specific power diesel car engine.

After Leverton and his team made a sortie to the Bonneville Speed Week in August that year, the work rate had ramped up appreciably. The first JCB444-LSR engine ran on the test bed at Ricardo on 18 October 2005. At that stage the engine was still run upright, and produced good power figures, around 700bhp on 'red' fuel pumps. There were signs of imminent power restrictions, however, as these pumps could not get sufficient fuel into the engine to develop more power.

Other, more pressing problems arose around this time. Beasley and Penny began to experience pistons 'picking up' in their bores, resulting in seizure. And then, when the decision had been taken to lay the engine on its side at an angle of 10° from the horizontal (to reduce the frontal area and centre of gravity of the car), the new dry sump lubrication system began to show signs of inability to scavenge and separate the oil and air effectively.

The pistons were always one of the biggest risk areas, since Ricardo was running an aluminium component at very, very high thermal and mechanical loads, and aluminium normally degrades rapidly in such extreme circumstances. But the material was essential to minimise weight, which would help the engine to run at almost twice its normal speed. The piston problem was also a corollary of the fuel system that was necessary to achieve the high power output that was needed.

In a petrol engine it is relatively easy to use fuel as a coolant. In some high performance turbocharged applications, it is common to put up with high consumption and alleviate thermal problems by spraying the pistons with fuel to keep them cool and prevent them from melting. All that would do in a turbocharged diesel application, however, would be to make smoke. Using fuel as a coolant was thus not an option.

'Because of that we inherently run very hot,' Penny explained. 'The old turbocharged Formula One engines were very well engineered, but there wasn't anything special to stop the pistons melting, just lots of fuel. In a port-injected petrol

↓ **Pistons were crucial components as the power output rose dramatically. Beasley shows Sir Anthony Bamford one of the successful profiles generated by Ricardo's expert, Dave Lee. To the left is JCB's director of engines, Alan Tolley.**

engine you inject fuel into the port or manifold over about 200 or 300 crank degrees. It evaporates, it gets sucked in, induction, compression, all nicely mixed, spark, burn. We've got to inject within about 30 crank degrees, you've got to inject the mix and burn it within about 50 crank degrees, that's what makes it a challenge with the fuel system. You need to put a hell of a lot of fuel in, in a very, very short space of time, and you've got to put it through a minute orifice to get the fuel to mix. Diesel fuel is not as prone to mixing as petrol because it's a heavy fuel so it doesn't evaporate, so you don't have the time to do that and you have to inject it through a tiny pinprick hole at massive pressure in a tiny space of time. That's why the fuel system on any diesel engine is a major challenge.'

Getting the piston to live, reliably, took a great deal of effort on behalf of Ricardo's expert Dave Lee. 'We "picked up" quite a few in the bores and it took a lot of the piston expertise that we have to sort that out,' Beasley admitted.

Lee worked through a number of piston profiles. With the original 108mm design the engine achieved almost 700bhp (680) in December 2005. But when they went to the 109mm Federal Mogul piston in February 2006, as the engine was inclined, the piston problems really began around the time that the troubleshooting focus also turned to the lubrication system. This was brand new, designed specifically for the 'laydown' engine installation and the resultant necessity for a dry sump system where oil was stored in a separate tank, both factors for which the original engine was not designed. The oil-scavenging shortfall was the principal problem. 'There is a huge amount of oil flow,' Penny explained. 'To control the piston there is something like a five or six times increase in oil cooling to it. You have got oil spraying the underside of the piston which then just creates a big foaming mess, so there is an awful lot of oil flow and over 5 bar boost. That means there is a huge amount of gas flow through the engine and latterly you get blow-by into the crankcase, so in terms of managing the dry sump system you have got an awful lot of oil and air flow.'

'We looked at the figures we were running, in terms of scavenge flow, air and oil, in relation to other people in

motorsport, and compared to Le Mans cars we were a factor of four or five times the flow,' Beasley added. 'We looked for some external advice, and the only people who had ever got anywhere near such flow and boost rates were the men who created the turbocharged Formula One engines in the '80s.'

By mid-May 2006 the 'laydown' JCB444-LSR engines were giving 610bhp reliably, although one of the four development 'mules' had suffered a failure (they were often run until they broke so that Ricardo could determine their limits – which proved surprisingly high). 'That isn't the power ceiling; development continues,' Leverton explained in one of the frequent technical meetings held that month at Visioneering. 'The 'old' (red) fuel pumps are maxed out, but 610bhp will be enough for the UK runway tests.'

The turbochargers had become the big issue at this stage. Ricardo was chasing supplier Garrett and had just discovered that a supplier to the American company that had previously promised castings eight weeks earlier, hadn't even started on them yet. Ricardo had gone elsewhere and the new units were expected by the end of that week. But there was still a problem. Ricardo had commissioned new castings, only to find that they needed recasting after Garrett had provided incorrect data. That was typical of the relatively small problems that beset such projects, and which can have serious repercussions. There was less than two months left in which to build the car, but as a result of this snafu designer John Piper at Visioneering still did not have the component he needed in order to validate the bracketry that would be required to install it in the car. It also meant a delay in getting a unit off to the supplier who would provide the heat insulation for the turbos.

Better news was just around the corner, however. That month Ricardo tried 'gold' fuel pumps for the first time. By then the piston profile had been finalised and the lubrication system developed, and they saw over 700bhp on the dyno for the first time.

Besides the four mule engines, another six had been built. The specification of Vehicle Engines 1 and 2, the so-called 'runway' engines, was frozen in May at 600bhp at 3,800rpm and 1,300Nm

of torque. Vehicle Engines 3 and 4, the so-called 'race' engines, would have 750bhp at 3,800rpm and 1,500Nm of torque. Two more 'short' engines were built up as spares for Bonneville. Each was individually calibrated to its fuel system, and all were balanced to within one per cent.

As the finishing touches were being put to the streamliner, the first pukka 'race' engine reached its 750bhp target output on Monday 10 July 2006. 'We could have done it earlier,' Penny suggested, 'but we had to validate the ice cooling and oil tank systems for the vehicle too, and provide supporting controls integration. It was a matter of prioritising things.'

The design finally chosen for the streamliner located one engine and transmission ahead of the driver's cockpit, the other behind it. There was no plan to have any mechanical link between the two, but rather to let the ground act as one. The gearshifts were synchronised, however.

'There is no need for an electronic link between the two engines, provided they produce similar power within an agreed level of tolerance,' Tim Leverton explained. 'In the event of one

engine failing, the car will automatically shift electronically into neutral as a safety default.

'We have talked this through quite a lot, and so long as the engines are close enough to each other in terms of their specific output and run at the same speed, they will regulate themselves mechanically.'

Nobody could foresee that a difference in output between the engines as they came on to boost would be the central mechanical problem that would have to be overcome.

Besides their phenomenal power and torque, there was another factor that surprised many when they studied the JCB444-LSR engine. Diesel engines had long had an image of being dirty and smelly – part of the thrill of watching the late Carl Heap's famed truck run at Bonneville was its huge cloud of black smoke – but very low emissions were a feature of the new racing powerplant. Ian Penny explained why.

'NOx emissions are a function of temperature and air/fuel ratio, and very much a local air/fuel ratio in the cylinder. In the classic diesel engine you inject the fuel and there is a small

**The horizontal engine installation (right and far right) made the car a little wider than typical Bonneville streamliners, but lowered the centre of gravity and enhanced the overall frontal area, boosting performance potential. It was a tight fit.**

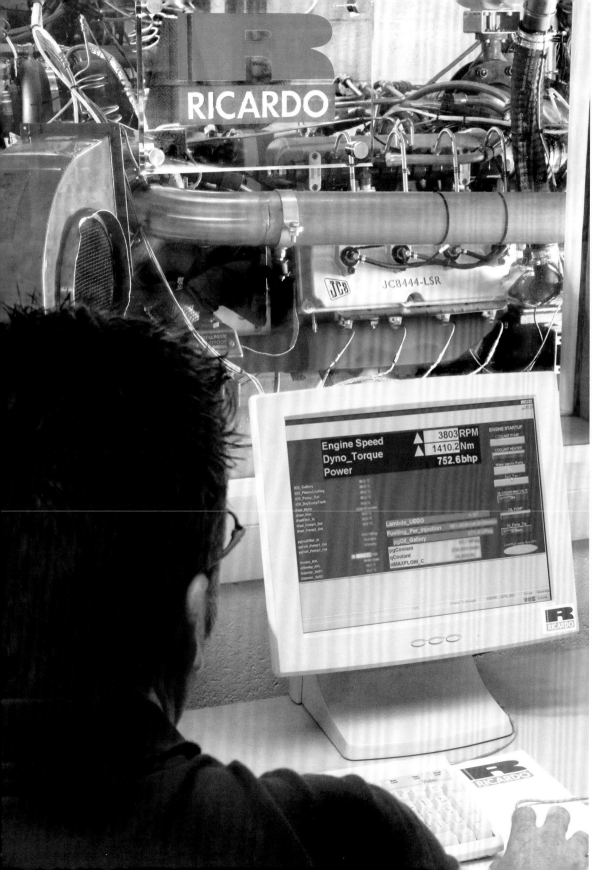

amount of mixing before combustions starts, called pre-mix, and then you get a diffusion burn as you inject it. Locally it is very, very rich. So when you look at a flame and it glows with that sort of yellowy colour, that's carbon being formed and then glowing. You form the carbon and then carbon burns and you get some residual, which is the smoke and the particulate.

'There are certain air/fuel ratios where you will make a lot of NOx, and those regions are exclusive. There are regions where you make NOx, regions where you make soot, and regions where you don't make anything. The whole thrust of combustion development on diesels is going to emissions-free combustion. It's what people call HCCI, or homogenous charge compression ignition. With compression-ignition typically you get very hot but you try to burn the diesel fuel at a much lower temperature and pressure.

'The JCB444-LSR engine runs a very low compression ratio, which brings the pressure and temperature down. It's 10.5 to 1, whereas a diesel is normally between 16 to 1 and 20 to 1. It's also got very, very high charge cooling so that the inlet manifold temperature is at 25 to 30°C, and that's after we have compressed it to 6 bar. So it's got very low pressure, very low temperature, it has water injection, which is a fantastic emissions control feature, and it runs a high pre-mix combustion system. So the kind of combustion we are operating is very much towards the future, HCCI low-temperature combustion. In other words, this is a very green engine.

'We are fully confident that it is easily going to be the most efficient land speed record car there's ever been. It is probably more fuel efficient running at motorway speeds than most passenger cars. Compared to a Formula One car it is three or four times the weight, twice the power and probably half the fuel consumption at 50 per cent higher speed.

'We are saying that you can go to the pinnacle of motorsport, and make a very high performance diesel that is very clean, very efficient and low carbon. People, particularly in the US, still have an old-fashioned view of diesel. Half the reason we wanted to be part of this project was to show that you can have the performance without compromising emissions or fuel consumption.'

# CHAPTER 5
# DEFINING THE CONCEPT

Several layout possibilities were investigated for Project H1. 'Starting in January 2005, we did a number of technical studies to see what the options were to package the engines, transmissions, wheels, driver, ice tanks, etc,' Matt Beasley explained. 'Some of the key decisions we had to make very early on were whether the engines were horizontal or vertical; and where the driver sat.'

They could locate him at the front of the car, with the two engines in line astern; effectively the Railton Special layout. But a cockpit mounted far forward makes it harder for a driver to detect incipient loss of traction, and there were safety implications. That also applied to the Goldenrod concept, with the engines in line in the middle of the car and the cockpit mounted behind the rear axle, dragster style. Putting the engines side by side, as George Eyston had with Thunderbolt and Mickey Thompson with Challenger, increased frontal area unnecessarily. Putting the cockpit in the middle, with one engine and transmission ahead of the driver and the other aft, as Thompson had on his Autolite Special, would put the main masses in the best places and locate the driver in the safest position within the vehicle structure.

'We also had the engine performance concept to define,' Beasley continued. 'What power did we need, how many engines was it going to take to achieve that? What boost level? And so on.'

Using a combination of engine and vehicle simulation, Ricardo prepared a presentation of sensitivity analysis, defining which areas were going to be critical: drag, frontal area, rolling resistance, vehicle mass. 'We were really setting targets for the main subsystems we had on the vehicle. So if we changed 10 per cent mass, what was the change in terms of power requirement? Or 10 per cent change in frontal area, and so on.' The initial weight target was 2,000kg but the end product, with driver, weighed between 2,600 and 2,700kg, though that was offset a little as the frontal area was reduced.

Initially they worked around Noble's estimate of tyre size based on 26.5in Mickey Thompson products.

'By the end of February we were keeping the car narrow, the engines were still vertical, and the driver was located at the front with ice tanks laid out down either side of the car,' Ian Penny said. 'One of the earliest concepts was that we would have an offset track, between front and rear, so that you don't have the rear wheels running in the same track as the front.'

By March things were looking a lot more like the final version of the car. The decision had been taken to incline the engines at 10 degrees from the horizontal. The vehicle thus became lower and a little wider, and the rear track was reduced as the front increased. The driver had finally been located in the mid position, after a key driver position meeting on 17 March 2005 with Andy Green, Matt Beasley and Ricardo's vehicle chief engineer Roland Jacob-Lloyd, who fulfilled the role that would eventually devolve to John Piper when Visioneering was chosen to build the car.

'We evaluated criteria in terms of risk, ride quality, driver view, vibration and so on, and demonstrated that we had pursued a logical path in order to decide where we were going to sit the driver and that it was the best position overall,' Beasley continued.

Leverton regarded this solution as 'absolutely fundamental' and 'blindingly obvious' from the liability point of view and had a

**Mike Turner, the JCB designer who created the handsome body of Dieselmax, discusses the streamliner's shape with Sir Anthony Bamford.**

**Brothers Bob and Bill Summers with their 409.277mph Goldenrod, one of the best-looking streamliners of all time, which located the former's cockpit behind the rear axle.**

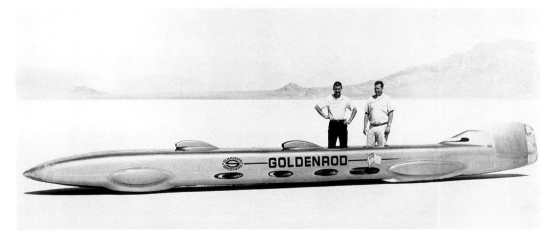

→ John Cobb sat right ahead of the front axle of his 403mph Railton Special. The layout made it particularly difficult to detect incipient wheelspin, especially on the rear axle.

↑ Mickey Thompson's 406mph 1959/60 Challenger used four Pontiac engines, mounted in side-by-side pairs in the centre of the car with the cockpit behind the rear axle.

↓ Thompson's subsequent 1968 Autolite Special used two Ford engines, one mounted ahead of the central cockpit, the other aft; this was the layout that Dieselmax would copy.

lively debate about it with Noble, who favoured the rear cockpit. When Green came aboard he had immediately said, 'Centre position...'

Shortly after that meeting the outline concept was effectively frozen.

One problem that arose was the case of the nine-foot driver. Ricardo sent Green a list of personal measurements it required, but as Beasley recalled: 'It was things like elbow to hand, shoulder to elbow and so on, and he did them but did them sort of inclusive rather than joint to joint as on our mannequin. We all looked at this in our meeting and said, 'He looks a bit big.' Then

somebody went away and stood the Andy Green measurement mannequin upright and actually measured it, and it was the best part of nine feet tall...' At six feet four inches, however, Green still occupied a substantial part of the machine.

At this stage the concept included a rudimentary chassis design, with ice tanks front and rear and the monocoque from a Lola Champ Car forming the driver's safety cell. Since they wanted to run at Bonneville Speed Week they had to have a basic steel spaceframe chassis into which they installed the carbon composite tub; the rules for Speed Week preclude pure-composite chassis.

Ricardo had access to an analysis Ayers had made long ago, before he even got involved with ThrustSSC. It was this investigation that had brought him into Noble's orbit in the first place. Ayers had long believed that many record breakers had underperformed, given their disparate specifications, and had set out to find out precisely why.

'He did his analysis and we did a lot of vehicle simulation which included what sort of gear ratios we needed and acceleration times at speed,' Beasley said. 'The two approaches correlated pretty well. And when we were out at Bonneville for the 2005 Speed Week we did a lot of measurements on the salt to validate some of the key assumptions used within these analyses.'

He recalled a series of braking g tests with a chuckle. 'We were driving along at 70mph on the road leading up to the pits, then putting the brakes on as hard as we could. We got a few heads turning even though we were trying to do it at quiet moments, but we managed over 30 friction tests. Jon Oakey and I had taken a g-meter out with us, and used it to record the deceleration during the brake tests. We then found a few different tarmac surfaces around Wendover and repeated that. The lowest salt mu – that's coefficient of friction – was about 0.55, the highest we measured anywhere on the flats was 0.85, so the average we used in our performance simulations was about 0.65 to 0.7. People reckon on a really good year it's much closer to 1.0 on the salt, which is what we measured on the tarmac.'

This was one of the most dynamic phases of the project as the vehicle concept was refined, with Ricardo working closely with Ron Ayers as he worked on his computational fluid dynamics research

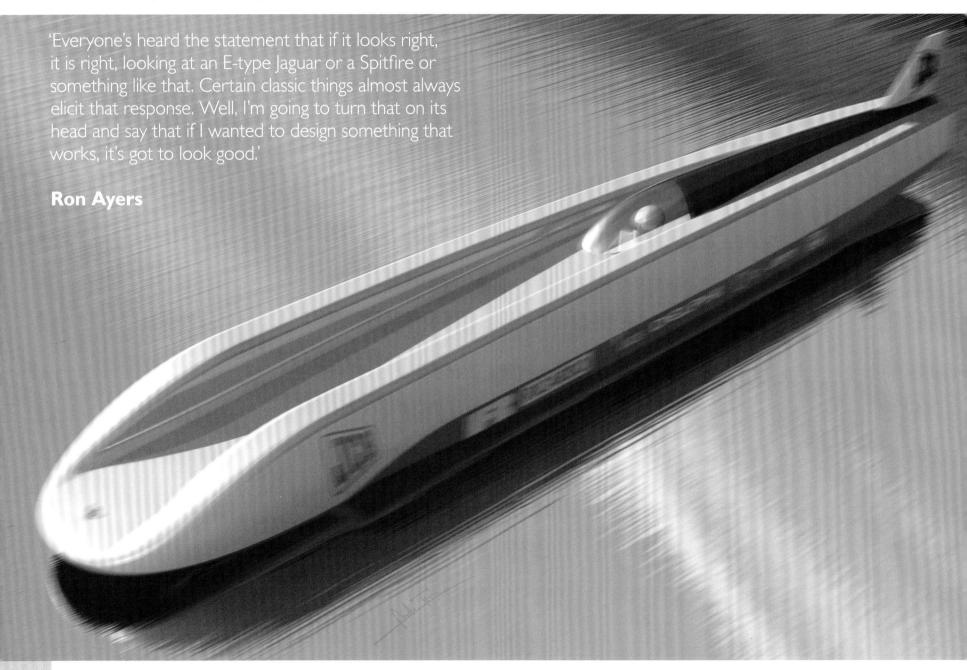

Mike Turner's original shape, based on Ricardo's preliminary concept, featured a higher wing line because of the 26.5-inch Thompson tyres, but bore more than a passing resemblance to the final product.

'Everyone's heard the statement that if it looks right, it is right, looking at an E-type Jaguar or a Spitfire or something like that. Certain classic things almost always elicit that response. Well, I'm going to turn that on its head and say that if I wanted to design something that works, it's got to look good.'

**Ron Ayers**

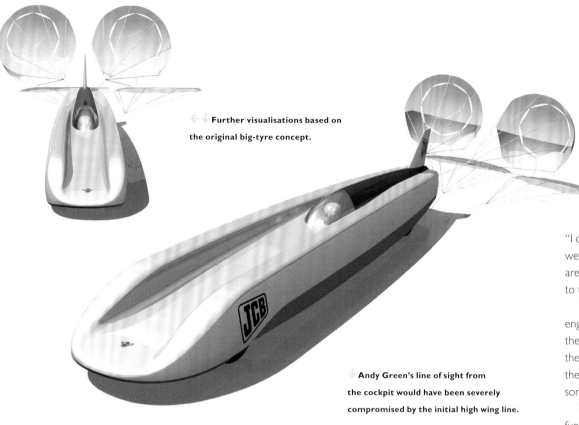

**Further visualisations based on the original big-tyre concept.**

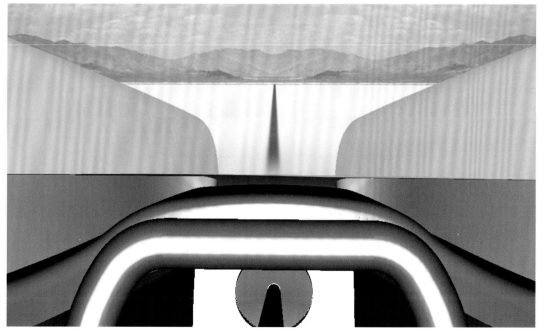

**Andy Green's line of sight from the cockpit would have been severely compromised by the initial high wing line.**

programme to define the aerodynamics. Essentially, CFD is a branch of fluid mechanics in which numerical methods and algorithms are used to investigate fluid flows.

'Ron was involved from Day One,' Beasley said. 'We had all these slices through the car and we had the challenge of what we wanted to fit in each slice of the car mechanically, and then Ron had his criteria such as, "I don't want this slice to change too much to the next, so really we want to squeeze that one but there'll be more room in the mid area of that one." So we would reiterate by looking at what we had to fit in there and how could we change the packaging.'

Once they had formulated the concept of mid-driver, horizontal engines and transmissions each end, offset tracks and 26.5in tyres, the shape and dimensions were more or less governed by that and the profile of the nose and other fine tuning was all that was left on the upper half of the car. But Ayers would break new ground with some very clever ideas about the underside.

When the time finally came to reveal the results of all this fundamental research to outsiders, JCB's industrial designer Mike Turner loved to pull his abracadabra moment. His laptop screen would display the image of the streamlined car – all yellow and black and long and sexy and, well, outrageously beautiful.

Ayers explained how he and Turner had generated the shape. 'Mike and his boss Gary Majors came to see Richard and I back in March 2005. Richard gave them the full treatment and showed them the ThrustSSC video and the book.

'Then we started on what the car should look like. I did some initial sketches, but I could see a problem. They had never designed anything like this, they designed tractors; they were 140 miles north of me, so I couldn't micro-manage them if I wanted to and I wasn't sure that was a good idea anyway. It was a JCB project, not my project. But I wanted to get the JCB input into it as soon as possible.

'So we agreed general specification such as the size of the wheels that things had to be fitted around, and then I said, "I could give you lots of detail, but I'm going to do something very different. Everyone's heard the statement if it looks right, it is right, looking at an E-type Jaguar or a Spitfire or something like that. Certain classic

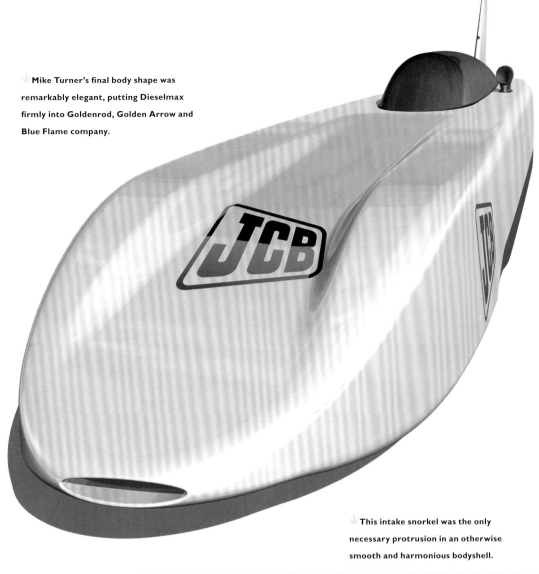

things almost always elicit that response. Well, I'm going to turn that on its head and say that if I wanted to design something that works, it's got to look good." And in aerodynamics, I think there's quite a lot in that. "What I'm saying is that, as skilled designers, if you use your judgement in designing a streamline shape I don't think it's going to be unaerodynamic. So design the most beautiful car in the world, one that will make photographers vie with one another. Then I will check it afterwards."

'When they had this brief, their faces lit up. Tim Leverton said to me the next day, "I don't know what you told those two, but they are absolutely on fire!"

'That got Mike motivated and using his judgement, and broadly speaking the top of the vehicle is virtually as he drew it, albeit squeezed a little. The bottom is the bit that I effectively micro-managed because that's directly related to get the computational fluid dynamics just right for the vertical forces and minimising the drag. As I say to people, the top side is for photographers, the underside is for engineers. All that beautiful shape on the top, that's all Mike.

'I've never tried to design like this before, but various other times I used the same ploy with JCB or Visioneering engineers, who liked to design wheel spats or intakes. I'd say the same thing: "You are an experienced engineer; use your judgement and I will then look at what you've done." And it always came up very close to the mark. So I turned that old phrase on its head and used it as a design tool. I think you can only do it with experienced designers. It solved three problems: I was too far away to micro-manage things; it ensured a good appearance; and, three, it got the JCB input at an early stage.'

It worked, both visually and aerodynamically.

This wasn't the only thing that Ayers did differently. Project HI broke new ground by record-breaking standards by ignoring wind tunnels completely. It was the first challenger whose aerodynamics were evolved exclusively via CFD.

'I cannot honestly say that I have broken new ground by relying totally on CFD, as I do not know about the research programmes of all the others,' he said with his habitual care. 'However, I suspect it is a first as CFD has only recently matured to a degree that

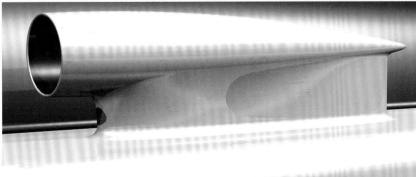

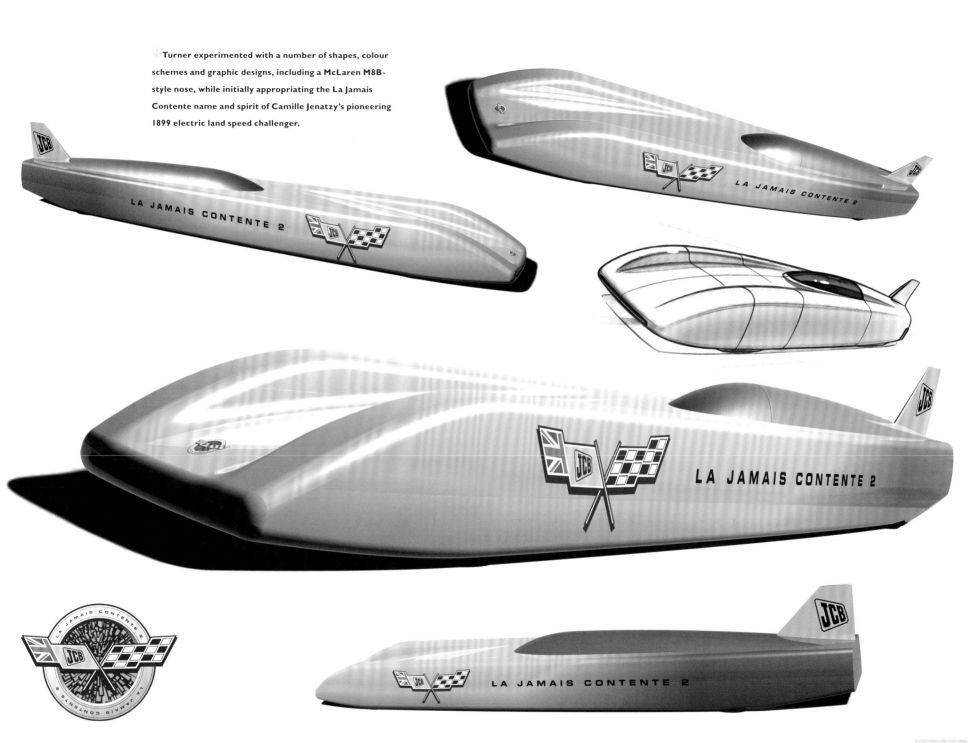

Turner experimented with a number of shapes, colour schemes and graphic designs, including a McLaren M8B-style nose, while initially appropriating the La Jamais Contente name and spirit of Camille Jenatzy's pioneering 1899 electric land speed challenger.

**Dieselmax was the first land speed car designed purely via computational fluid dynamics. The red indicates high pressure areas, blue low, with green in between.**

makes it relatively trustworthy. Many predecessors, of course, did not use any research at all. They just put their foot down, and would no doubt consider my activities as being against the hallowed traditions of record breaking. Indeed, when I showed my ThrustSSC CFD pictures to Art Arfons in 1997 he said I was "spoiling the fun for us old country boys". He did not seem impressed by the argument that my technology could keep them alive while they had their fun.'

Ayers had good reason for relying on CFD. First, there was the Mach number problem. At 350mph a vehicle is travelling at a Mach number of about 0.46. In others words, at 46 per cent of the speed of sound. Even at that speed, compressibility effects are beginning to become significant. Indeed, in the region near the wheel/ground contact point the flow locally actually goes supersonic. Such effects could not be simulated in a low-speed wind tunnel with a rolling road. The second reason was one of scale. To fit a long, slender vehicle into a tunnel with a rolling road would mean being restricted to a model scale of about one-sixth. With the rolling road tunnels that were available to the team, they would also be restricted to an airflow of about one-fifth of vehicle speed. Multiplying the two together (to get the true viscous flow scale effect) meant that they would be in error by a factor of 30. This would make the boundary layer around the vehicle very non-representative. As the ground clearance was not much greater than the boundary layer thickness, serious errors could occur in flow pattern.

'When we did ThrustSSC, CFD was a very immature technology that no one trusted,' Ayers added. 'My rocket sled tests were among the first experiments that showed CFD in a good light. There is now much more evidence that it works.'

Back then, Ayers carried out simultaneous CFD and real-time tests with a scale model mounted on a rocket sled fired to supersonic speeds; the findings from the two programmes had an almost identical correlation, and on that basis Noble and Ayers proceeded with ThrustSSC.

When it was suggested that Ayers should also use wind tunnel tests as a confirmation for Project H1, he replied that if the two methods disagreed, he would, in this instance, trust the CFD over the wind tunnel, so there was no point.

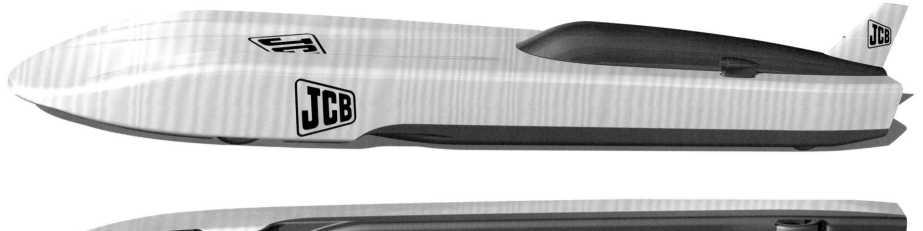

Ayers stipulated three clear aerodynamic requirements. The first was minimal drag. This was an obvious requirement, but since skin friction drag has a significant effect on performance it was clear that the overall surface area must be minimised, as well as the frontal area. The CFD showed that skin friction drag accounted for some 60 per cent of the total drag, with the profile drag only about 40 per cent. This dominance of viscous phenomena confirmed the importance of getting the correct boundary layer profile, and hence the correct scale. Turner's beautiful upper body shape effectively shrink-wrapped itself over the mechanicals in such a way that each contour passed smoothly into the next. And as a result of his analysis of underperformance, Ayers paid very close attention to airflow beneath the car.

The second thing was to control downforce. Significant aerodynamic lift would clearly be dangerous, and would also lead to reduced traction because of resultant tyre slippage. However, too much downforce would be just as damaging since it would increase rolling resistance. Ayers thus aimed for almost zero lift and zero downforce, seeking to create a neutral shape. Research indicated that the aerodynamic drag was so low that, he estimated, it was significantly less than the rolling resistance.

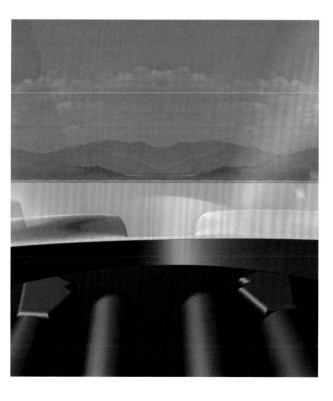

↑ **Final body shape shows (top) Mike Turner's 'beautiful bit' and (below) Ron Ayers' 'technical bit', with his spray drag-defeating 'racetrack' between the front wheels clearly visible.**

← **With the 23-inch Goodyear tyres, Green's line of sight from the cockpit was dramatically improved.**

'At least part of the rolling resistance is caused by particles of salt being kicked up by the front of the vehicle, and impinging on the rear,' he explained. 'I have coined the term "spray drag" by analogy with the spray drag experience with record-breaking boats. Having recognised the phenomenon during my ThrustSSC research, I have tried to minimise it here. No one else, as far as I know, has tried this, so I have no idea how well it will work. To this extent, we are doing genuine research.'

To minimise this spray drag the underside of the car was very carefully sculpted not just in the area of the spats around the lower section of the wheels, but also where the air flowed through the choke points between the front and rear wheels. Spray beneath the front of the car was deflected out to the side via sculpted channels located just behind the front wheels, to ensure that the rear wheels and tyres could run on as clean a surface as possible.

The air flowing under the car accounted for about half of the total aerodynamic drag – as well as controlling the spray drag. 'I am sure the photographers will be interested in the top view,' Ayers reiterated. 'But the real technical challenge is on the underside.'

The final requirement was yaw stability. Clearly, the back end of the car had got to stay at the back. If the vehicle was envisaged as an arrow or a dart, it was the tail fin that acted as the flights to minimise yaw and maintain aerodynamic stability at maximum speed.

Since the car was created along Formula One lines, with the aerodynamic profile having priority, there could have been some friction between Ayers and chief designer John Piper and his design team. It said much for their respective personalities that this never arose. 'If there was any variance between the way Ron approached his side of the task with the aerodynamics, and we handled the build programme,' Piper said, 'it was merely a cultural difference. Ron is a delight and it is a privilege to know him and to work with him. His approach was to be as helpful to our packaging as possible: "What do I need to fit the shape round?" Ours was the opposite tack! "Ron, tell us what shape you want and we'll get the package inside it."

'In a Formula One team efficiency is what it's all about. You spend a lot of money trying to provide the engineering to deliver

To facilitate access to the cockpit, the entire canopy was hinged forward.

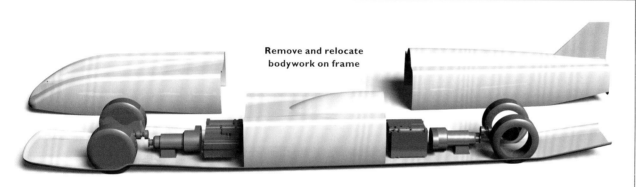

Remove and relocate bodywork on frame

Front locating pins?

Undertray remains in position

Front and rear bodywork location using mechanical fasteners

Rear locating pins?

Right-hand side – 'Dirty' side – exhaust outlets etc

Left-hand side – 'Clean' side – used for brochure shots etc

Hard-point in bodywork for driver entry and egress

Mike Turner's original drawings and notes indicate the thinking that went into aspects such as accessibility to the cockpit and mechanical components during the design of the bodyshell.

The decision to integrate the livery of Green's helmet (final design on left) was another sign of the project's professionalism, and the work was carried out by the experienced Mike Fairholme.

The final body shape emerges dramatically in full scale.

that. The problem is that nobody has done this type of record car before, so you can't walk down the pit lane and go, "Ooh, that's a good idea." And there are no regulations that guide you. There aren't any markers anywhere. The only markers really are the laws of physics. But that's what makes it so exciting.'

To facilitate visualisation of the overall car, Piper's team generated a highly detailed 3D electronic computer model revealing all of its components to help to identify the fit and practicality of each in relation to the others. A full-size chassis mock-up was then built for final verification of all aspects of the concept before work started on the real version.

A conventional water-cooling radiator would have created too much aerodynamic drag so there was a traditional land speed racing cooling system based initially around two 100-litre water and ice tanks. The system made use of the latent heat required to melt the ice in addition to the low temperature of the water, and this meant that the only intakes the car needed were a narrow cooling slot in the nose and a snorkel intake on one flank to feed the rear engine.

The overall result of the collaboration between Ayers and Turner was an outstandingly beautiful and effective car with a CdA (drag coefficient) less than 0.15, extraordinary even by land speed record standards, but especially in one that was wider than conventional wheel-driven streamliners.

As it happened, one morning at Bonneville Speed Week the announcer said: 'I don't want to be treading on anyone else's toes by saying this,' as Dieselmax came to the start line, 'but this is the most beautiful car on the track.'

Ayers also liked what JCB had done with the colour scheme, blending its traditional yellow with sufficient black to enhance rather than overstate the streamliner's elegance.

'The other satisfying thing was when I met Sir Anthony, and he just said, "It looks gorgeous!" I thought, "If the boss thinks that way, we've scored!"'

There was just one problem, and it threatened to throw the entire project into crisis. At a technical review meeting in November 2005, John Piper told everyone that what they had was not going to work. It was too heavy, too big, and too slow.

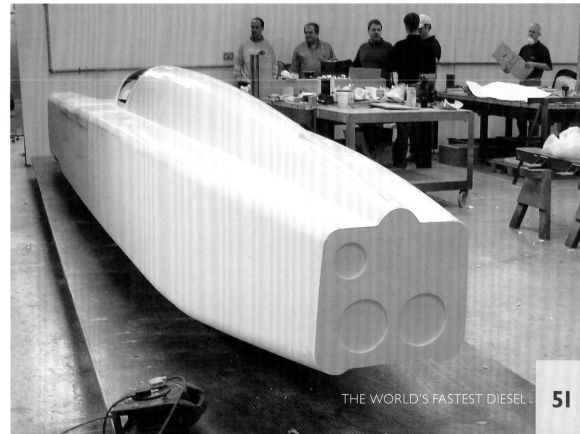

# CHAPTER 6

# A RACE AGAINST TIME

Record-breaking cars habitually have lengthy gestation periods, mainly because the finance is not there to do the job in a hurry. Richard Noble, for example, started building his Thrust2 and ThrustSSC cars without any safety net of adequate funding, chasing it on the hoof while his designers and build teams started work. The Thrust2 programme was launched in October 1977 and the finished car first ran at Bonneville in September 1981. Likewise, the ThrustSSC programme began in 1994 but the car did not run until 1996.

JCB had all the funding it needed right from the start, but its machine had to be designed and created in no more than eight months. And when John Piper looked closely at the concept model, he was unimpressed.

Piper had been in the party that Tim Leverton had taken on an explorative sortie to Speed Week at Bonneville in August 2005.

'It was a secret mission,' Leverton recalled. 'Me, Allan Tolley and Dave Brown from JCB, Richard and Andy, Jon Oakey and Matt Beasley from Ricardo, and John Piper from Visioneering. I was incognito – I wore my shades and sunblock all the time!

'Well, if you want to go incognito to Bonneville, don't take Richard or Andy! The first morning we turned up, looking dead cool, the first person we had a chat with was streamliner driver Earl Wooden. And the first thing he says is, "Hey, Richard, Andy, I hear you're doing a twin-engined diesel streamliner..." So much for secrecy!

'Bonneville is such an open community. They told us all we wanted to know. And we caught our own first dose of salt fever.'

Bonneville effectively marked the end of Ricardo's involvement with the vehicle, as opposed to the engines, and was where Beasley first met Piper. Visioneering was one of the companies invited to quote for the design and build business. Lola Cars was another, while Noble favoured John Biddlecombe, formerly of G-Force, who had built the chassis for ThrustSSC.

Leverton had wanted a third alternative which would give JCB more management control than going to a turnkey manufacturer. Piper was there because Leverton had decided to go with Visioneering, though the order had not yet been given to the company pending Sir Anthony Bamford's final approval of the project.

Based in Coventry, Visioneering supplied expertise, technology and project management for the automotive, aerospace and manufacturing industries, and was experienced in automotive tooling, design engineering and parts manufacture. Its client list included many top automotive marques and aerospace manufacturers.

Leverton already knew Brian Horner and John Piper. 'When Brian came back to me he put forward John to be the car designer. It was an inspired choice that he (Brian) could not have realised the significance of when he made it.'

**Humour didn't take long to surface once people started mixing together at Humphrey Walters' team-building exercise in May 2006.**

The first stage of construction entailed building a prototype chassis so that all components could be trial-fitted before the pukka version was finalised.

Leverton first met Piper in the pits at Le Mans in 1997, where Piper was running the Panoz GTR car he had designed for Reynard. Leverton much admired the front-engined machine and later got Piper Design to do some work for Rolls-Royce, as he also admired his specialisation in mechanisms (such as the Virgin business-class seat) and his innate sense of high quality.

'Even though Visioneering had never made a racing car at that stage, I had the most confidence that we could make it work with them. Clearly I have no regrets at all now!'

Leverton now felt that he had struck a good balance between JCB control and involvement, Ricardo engagement and clear responsibilities for Visioneering. While Ricardo would continue to develop the engines in conjunction with JCB's own transmission engineers, Visioneering would take over responsibility for the chassis, suspension and brakes, the carbon-fibre composite bodyshell, the powertrain installation, and the car control systems. It would also take a leading role during testing and development and during the record attempt itself.

Piper would lead the team as chief designer, bringing in people such as engineer John Bingham, Alastair Macqueen, who had wide experience with teams such as Eddie Jordan Racing, Jaguar and Bentley in motorsport, and Duffy Sheardown who cut his teeth with Andrea Moda in F1.

Piper himself was vastly experienced, having worked with Williams, Benetton and Team Lotus in F1, been technical director at Reynard Racing Cars and Prodrive, and chief designer at TWR Jaguar, whose 1990 V12 XJR-9 won the Le Mans 24 Hour race before Piper's 1991 XJR-14 won the World Sports Car Championship.

'At the end of September I got a hurried call from Dave Brown,' Piper said. 'We'd got the project. We were all raring to go, to be getting on with things given the limited timescale. And I remember saying to Dave Brown, "Great, we'll start Monday!" and he said, "Well, no, the factory is on shutdown for a week." That just blew my brains out!' The deal with Visioneering was finally agreed on 17 October.

Leverton remembered: 'Once John came aboard it was essential that he felt that he really had the authority and responsibility to make the detailed design decisions on the car. I knew he would have to start from scratch and I fully expected him to do so because only if you do that can you be the master of the engineering of something as complex as this. The chief designer has to own the decisions that are made. He cannot come back at the end when it doesn't work and say, "But I didn't agree with that." So we said, "You're the car man," and took a step away and let him do his job.'

'I was a bit taken aback to begin with,' Piper revealed, 'because we'd been led to believe that the detailed design was done and none of it was! I thought I was going to do three days a week, helping to make the car. I ended up working 12-hour days from the start, and 14-hour days eventually.

'Anyhow, in October 2005 I started to put a team together. In the belief that we needed suspension and good vehicle dynamics, I recruited John Bingham because he is fantastic on that.'

But there was a problem.

'I didn't like the concept chassis design, I didn't feel that the suspension that had been drawn up would work, and the 50:50 weight distribution wouldn't work under acceleration. You need front weight bias for stability.

'The original concept used two three-speed JCB gearboxes with torque converters, which would hurt acceleration. They were huge and heavy. I also thought that the weight and drag figures used in the simulations were a bit optimistic. I didn't believe we could achieve the CdA target with a car of that cross-section.

'I got John (Bingham) to create a technical specification and we began to take control of the engineering meetings. Data for simulation from then on would come from our technical specification. John and I had fed our figures into the simulation and there was a meeting in November where we told everyone that as things stood the car would only be able to do 300mph. There were sharp intakes of breath around the table.

'We needed to reduce the cross-section, so we narrowed the tracks front and rear, we put Andy in a seating buck and managed to drop the height of the canopy, and then we started to get some decent CFD figures. There were two ice tanks at that stage,

Observing the SCTA-BNI rules regarding chassis, Piper opted for a 50mm square-tube fabricated design. Corus helped by coming up with the right gauge steel so he could design a structure stiff enough to achieve a torsional resonance frequency well above the wheel frequency, for an overall weight of 250kg.

front and rear; we put just one, in the nose, and moved each engine forwards, to get closer to ideal weight distribution. That improved things to the point where we'd get over 300mph, but only around the 330mph mark, so we really set about the cross-section and packaging space, and made it all much tighter. We also shortened the car to save weight.

'The biggest problem was the three-speed gearboxes, and our simulation showed for a start that you'd need at least four, probably five gears. So we started to look at something different, a race car transaxle. We chose one from Xtrac. I was told at one stage not to consider this as being like a race car!'

Dumping the three-speed gearboxes realised a massive weight saving because there were now no propshafts – the original final drive had been connected to the gearboxes by Hooke-jointed propshafts.

The engines were rubber-mounted, and and it was thought that this would shake the car to pieces and wouldn't allow the ride height adjustment that was necessary.'

Piper also did not want the 26.5in tyres, and thought that the only valid option was the smaller 23in Goodyears. 'John and I were insistent that we had to have control of the tyre validation programme. I knew that Richard Noble was dead against the Goodyears, but I didn't regard any of the feedback I heard on them as anything but hearsay and anecdotal evidence.

Corus came up with the right gauge 50mm square tube steel from which John Piper's first spaceframe chassis was fabricated.

'We thus made several decisions, not all of which were popular. We would have to validate the smaller tyres, because they were our only chance of creating the cross-section we needed to deliver the right aerodynamic performance. We would mount the engines rigidly to get the stiffness we needed in a new chassis structure to achieve decent suspension dynamics; and have a race car transaxle to deliver the weight we needed.'

Thus, in November 2005 the project fell into crisis. Visioneering started doing computer-aided design (CAD) schemes from October, but was unable to start drawing anything until the third week in January 2006. 'We were supposed to freeze the package that month but we were nowhere near being able to do that because we were still playing with the configuration of the car. All we could do was freeze the design solutions then and let the packaging shake out as we started drawing the car in detail, because the engine installation was still changing.'

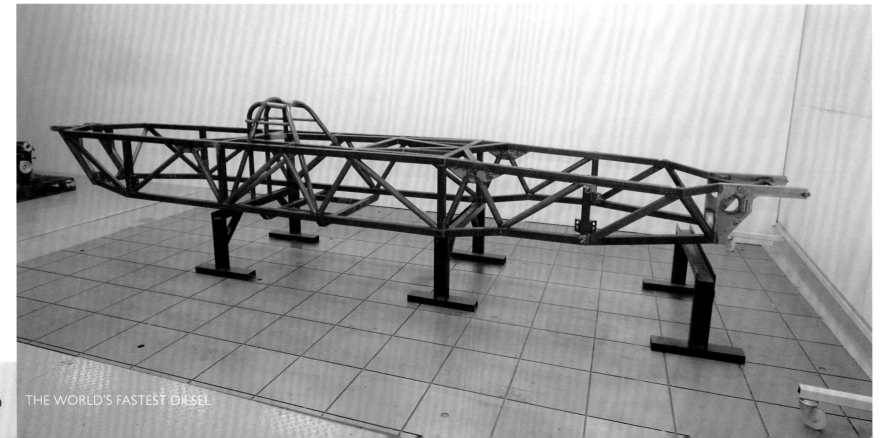

The final concept was eventually frozen in February 2006 after the final CFD pass, and the first detailed drawings didn't go out until March.

'I also insisted on a rigid powertrain and final drive unit because it would help to stiffen the car and react the drive torque through the gearbox casing rather than through the chassis, which made a big difference to the car's behaviour.

'We also took the opportunity, with the very short suspension wishbones, to keep the geometry as perfect as we could. We mounted the suspension on a subframe and pivoted the engine with it when making the ride-height adjustment, as this was the only way we could accommodate the tyre size we might end up with. But the reality was that only the 23in tyres would work. We really stuck our necks out there because they were our only chance. John and I knew that if the Goodyears didn't work, we didn't have a car.'

Observing the legal requirements of the Southern California Timing Association (SCTA) and Bonneville Nationals Inc (the organisers of Speed Week at Bonneville) for a steel spaceframe chassis, Piper opted for a 50mm square-tube fabricated design. Corus helped by coming up with the right gauge steel so he could design a structure stiff enough to achieve a torsional resonance frequency well above the wheel frequency. It was also the most cost-efficient way of producing a vehicle that had to be both prototype and finished product, since it allowed changes to made much more simply.

The cockpit safety cell was a bespoke carbon fibre composite monocoque structure with mandatory SCTA steel tube rollover cage, and a 15-litre wedge-shaped fuel cell was located behind the driver's seat.

A three-piece composite underfloor completed the basic structure, lending it further stiffness by being bolted and bonded to the bottom of the chassis.

The engineers had to figure out the best way to install the JCB444-LSR engines in the chassis, and to design the ice cooling system that was needed to provide the significant heat rejection that was required. The single tank in the nose would be packed with 180kg of regular cocktail ice cubes before 20 litres of cold

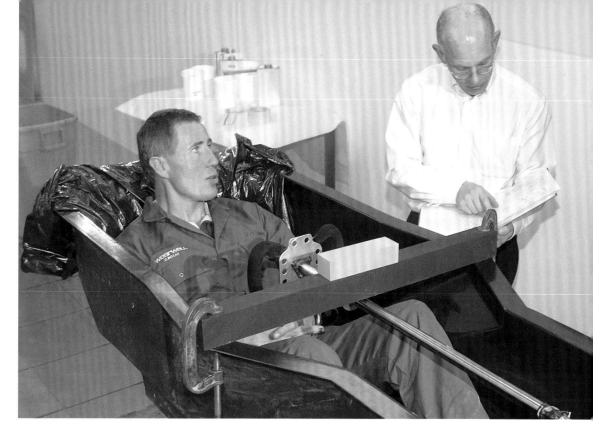

water were pumped in. With each run lasting around 90 seconds, the streamliner would convert this mix to warm water and the system had to be drained, flushed and refilled after each one.

JCB engineers David Hoyle and Simon Evans took responsibility for the transmissions, which comprised Xtrac six-speed transaxles and JCB stepper boxes between each engine and gearbox. Gearshifting was via a steering-wheel-mounted paddle-shift mechanism, while torque tubes and oil-immersed multi-plate clutches transmitted the power. Traction control was not used, not just because it is outlawed by SCTA-BNI regulations but also because the aim was to keep the car as simple as possible and because the anticipated low friction (mu factor approx. 0.6) of the salt would probably preclude the sort of very hard acceleration which might induce wheelspin.

To Andy Green's relief a conventional rack and pinion system steered the front wheels (as opposed to the rears on ThrustSSC). There was no power-assistance, again to keep things simple and because it was not believed necessary given the relatively small angles of input Green would have to make, and the chosen ratio gave him seven degrees of lock. It was expected that this would generate a turning circle of around a quarter of a mile and at one

**Andy Green has a seat fitting in the carbon-fibre cockpit, as race engineer Alastair Macqueen liaises with him on the locations of key controls.**

Body panels for the streamliner
take shape on a special buck, prior to
manufacture in carbon-fibre composite.

Eoin Corrigan's fabrication skills were
always much in demand.

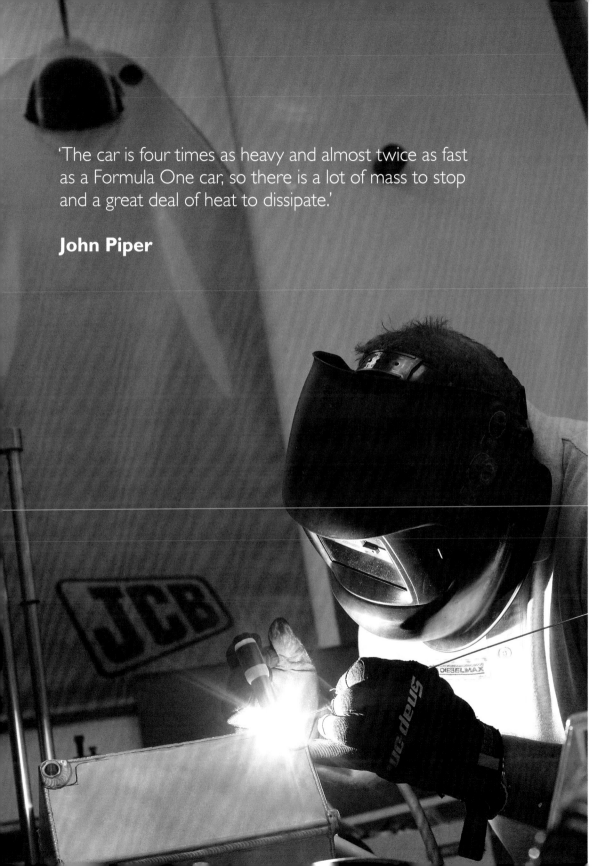

'The car is four times as heavy and almost twice as fast as a Formula One car, so there is a lot of mass to stop and a great deal of heat to dissipate.'

**John Piper**

One of the most complex and important areas was the braking system. Adhering religiously to the default-to-safety philosophy, there were three separate systems comprising dual-circuit friction brakes on all four wheels, driver-activated exhaust braking, and parachutes.

The switch to 23in tyres on 15in wheels meant that a conventional braking system was not an option. An F1 car brake would be too small, a Champ Car disc too big. 'John Bingham's lovely suspension geometry meant that the lower pick-up point went so far into the wheel that there was no room for the brake,' Piper explained. 'So I started thinking aircraft brakes, an inside-out brake.'

The system he came up with used carbon brake rotors clamped not by conventional six-pot racing calipers but instead by brake pistons mounted within the wheel upright. The pistons were activated by a torque tube which pushed them hydraulically into contact with a stator that clamped the rotor, which was keyed into the wheel that Piper designed. These wheels would rotate at 5,500rpm or twice the speed of a Formula One car's.

In the past several land speed cars had fried their brakes at anything over 200mph, so this system, which boasted dramatically enhanced swept area and effectiveness, aimed to provide friction braking fully capable of stopping the car in an emergency, such as complete failure of the twin parachute back-up system.

'We went to see Dunlop and they said yes when we categorically asked them to do the complete system. Later they claimed they had not quoted to do certain parts of it and withdrew. There were a few nervous days as Tim Leverton and Dave Brown negotiated to pay Dunlop for work done and to buy the world's only carbon rotor blanks that they had. I then took them to Richard Bass at AP, showed him our CAD scheme, and in a really short time they took over the detailed drawings and finessed them, built the system and tested it on a rig.'

AP performed two full-speed stops within 50 minutes, thus confirming that the car could stop from 225mph on wheel brakes

stage the plan during turnarounds between each run was to lift the car and rotate it on a specially devised turntable. In practice, JCB Dieselmax could be turned in much smaller spaces. Thus the turnaround team would simply wheel it round.

Conventional heavy-duty wishbone suspension was specified front and rear, with coil springs and hydraulic dampers. Piper said: 'My overwhelming impression from the Bonneville trip was how bad the cars were at getting traction and getting their power down, at controlling wheel movement. It was a bad year for the salt, but they were all struggling. Their philosophy was that they could always come back the following year, but we wouldn't have that option. I come from the culture of cars with suspension, grip and traction, and decided all of these were important things and that our car had to have suspension. Ride-height adjustment is also important. We wouldn't have active ride, in the interests of keeping things simple, but there would be a range of adjustments. I knew we'd have a car similar to what other people were doing at Bonneville, with their advantage of experience, so what would be different is that we would build a fast one that could actually be driven fast.'

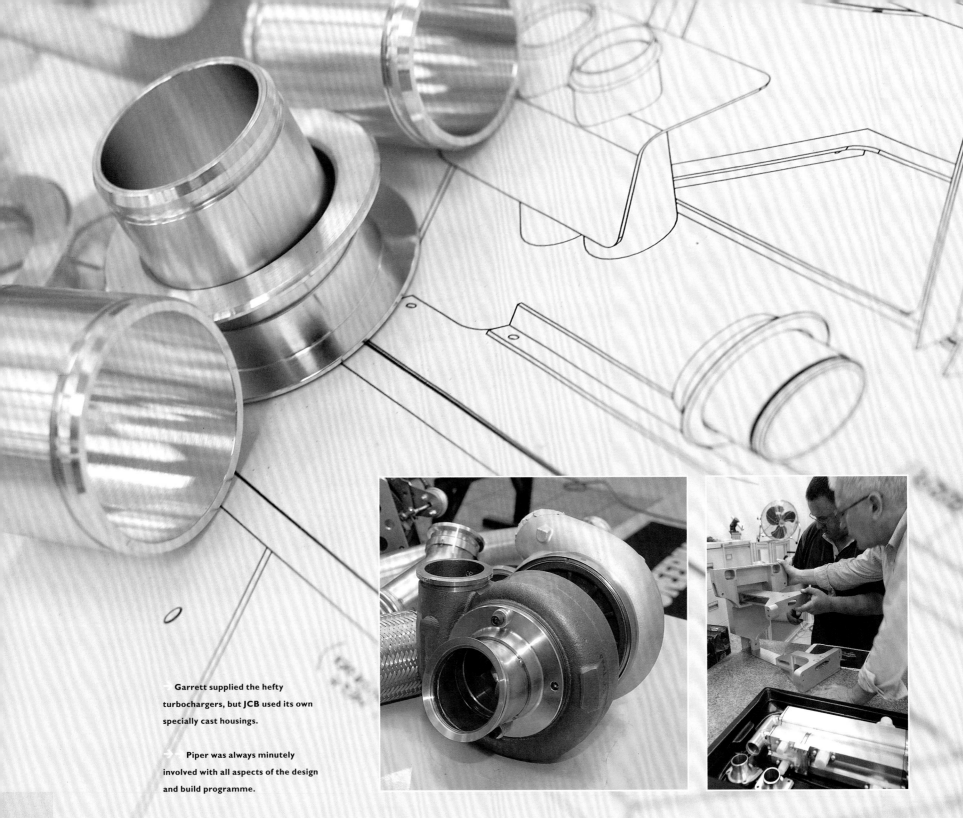

Garrett supplied the hefty turbochargers, but JCB used its own specially cast housings.

Piper was always minutely involved with all aspects of the design and build programme.

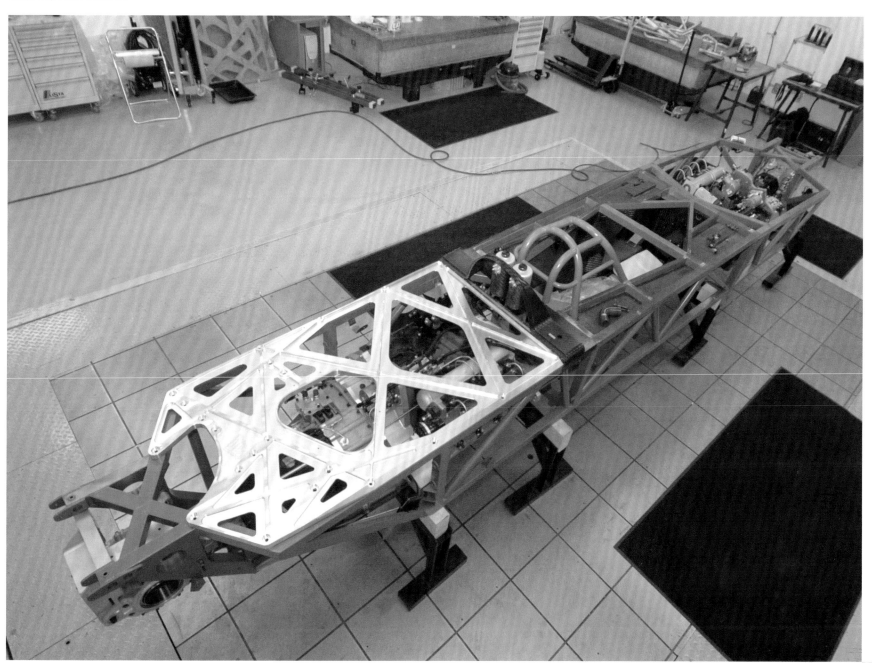

Overhead shot of the completed frame with both engines and transmissions installed gives an insight into the complexity of **JCB Dieselmax.**

alone, make a turnaround and do it again. If the parachute braking system failed, they could still get a record. If the wheel brakes were used at 280mph they would be history, but they could certainly avoid an accident even without any 'chutes.

The brakes were another area of controversy. Some people on the project deemed carbon brakes unnecessary, but without them the vital testing at both RAF Wittering and Wendover Airfield would not have been possible.

The exhaust brake was a proprietary US truck system comprising a simple butterfly in the exhaust pipe closed by a pneumatic cylinder, while there were two parachutes. Initially these were 40 sq ft on a 40ft tow line, but subsequently 30 sq

ft 'chutes on a 60ft line were used. Piper pointed out: 'The car is four times as heavy and almost twice as fast as a Formula One car, so there is a lot of mass to stop and a great deal of heat to dissipate.'

The greatest danger came when a vehicle was slowing down. In October 2002 71-year-old Nolan White had been killed while attempting to beat his own SCTA-BNI piston-engined wheel-driven record of 413mph set the previous August. On both occasions his Autopower/Parts Peddler streamliner lost all three braking 'chutes on return runs. In August, White steered on to soft salt and stopped safely; in October the car dug in and rolled at around 300mph, and he died three days later from head injuries.

↓ **The design of the cockpit layout, the dashboard and the choice of instrumentation owed a great deal to Andy Green's experience and input.**

It was easy for some to dismiss the JCB record attempt since it aimed for half the speed that Green had achieved with ThrustSSC. But Nolan White's death, besides dealing a shattering blow to the Bonneville community, was a painful reminder of the inherent risk in any land speed endeavour.

One of the reasons behind the success of the project lay in Piper's inherent calmness. There was the turbocharger problem to deal with at the technical meeting at the factory in May 2006. As Beasley reported on the previous night's failure of one of the development mules that part of the meeting was somewhat tense, as much of the news seemed negative. Piper alleviated things when he said: 'I'll tell you what we haven't done so far on the car, and fortunately that is a shorter list.'

Two chassis were built, the first a mock-up that would enable everything to be trial-fitted. While much of the car was designed on CAD, some things – such as hosework, pipework and the electrical loom – were best done for real on the actual mock-up, to save time. The build plan pivoted around having four weeks of activity on the car after the drivelines had been fitted. When the pukka chassis arrived on 5 June, Piper recalled, 'and all hell broke loose', the team put the car together in an astonishing six weeks, working flat-out through each of them.

By then, Project H1 had a new name. Fingal, the project's publicity and marketing partner, developed a shortlist from which one was chosen: the streamliner was now called JCB Dieselmax.

Just before it left for Bonneville, Brian Horner received a letter from Tim Leverton. 'To design a car capable of setting a new land speed record for a diesel-powered vehicle, including the integration of two JCB444-LSR engines developed at Ricardo, is one of the most complex engineering projects imaginable,' Leverton wrote. 'To have completed this task in just 10 months, and then to have the car meet all its initial development targets in just nine days from its first run, is a stunning achievement.

Visioneering's contribution provided the vital third side of the triangle. The fact that JCB, Ricardo and Visioneering all worked so closely was a cornerstone of the programme's eventual success.

# CHAPTER 7

# ROUND, BLACK AND TIRESOME

In a relative sense, Richard Noble and his Thrust teams had two luxuries in creating their cars to challenge the outright land speed record: they could use pure-thrust turbojet engines and therefore did not need to drive them through the wheels, and they could forget about rubber tyres and run on solid aluminium wheels.

JCB Dieselmax had no such fortune. The one thing that threatened the feasibility of the entire programme was tyre availability.

It soon became clear that the problem with buying 'off the peg' record tyres was that they often presented more questions than they answered, as their rotational and load-bearing capabilities were not always fully identified. That was why JCB engineer Dave Brown also found himself trawling the aircraft scrapyards of America early in the project's life in search of something seemingly elusive: a tyre that would hold together under the centrifugal force that JCB Dieselmax would encounter at speeds in excess of 300mph.

There had, of course, been tyres that had exceeded 600mph. Goodyear had successfully supplied both Craig Breedlove with his Spirit of America – Sonic 1, and Gary Gabelich's Blue Flame. When the rocket car achieved its 622.407mph in 1970 it marked the last time the outright world land speed record was broken using rubber tyres. But they were designed for a pure-thrust car which put no torque loading through the sidewalls. Such tyres would not necessarily be suitable for a heavier, wheel-driven automobile, and in any case they were no longer available.

Brown had discussions with a number of tyre companies, each of whom eventually declined to participate. Product liability issues in the US scared off most. Prior to June 2005 the French Michelin company had expressed interest, but then came the fiasco at the US Grand Prix at Indianapolis, where its 14 runners had to withdraw after the grid formation lap because their tyres proved dangerously unsuited to the demands of one particular banked corner; suddenly Michelin had myriad problems to consider in America and lost all interest in building tyres for a speed record attempt.

That was when Brown began to consider aircraft tyres. 'We looked at either Boeing 737 nose-wheel tyres or Falcon 500 main wheel tyres, rated at 225mph.' He needed tyre data that included maximum speed, load rating and running pressure; most proprietary Bonneville tyres come only with a speed rating and no further indication of how that speed was calculated. Not all aircraft tyres were fully specific, either. Eventually, proprietary 26.5in Mickey Thompson tyres seemed the most suitable.

Then, around November 2005, came the controversial decision to switch from them to 23in off-the-shelf Goodyears. 'It was decided that the aerodynamics were far more important than all the transmission work we had done,' Brown said. 'We had based our tyre size on transmission requirements, and now we had to get the smallest tyres.'

When the advance party had made its fact-finding trip to Speed Week in August 2005, it became clear that few Bonneville regulars liked the idea of running the small Goodyears. The Thompsons appeared to be the favoured tyre. Richard Noble certainly preferred them. But chief designer John Piper and

**600mph tyres were developed by Goodyear for Craig Breedlove's 1965 Spirit of America – Sonic 1, but were no longer available and in any case were designed for pure-thrust vehicles, not those which had to transmit drive through their wheels and tyres.**

The controversial decision to go for 23-inch Goodyear tyres (far right) necessitated bespoke aluminium wheels (above) and a bespoke mechanical braking system (top), but had a crucial effect on performance.

suspension specialist John Bingham were adamant: it had to be the Goodyears. There was no viable option.

'Goodyear rated its tyres at 300mph and 1,700lb,' Brown said. 'So we wouldn't be putting as much as 6,800lb through the four tyres when you'd taken into account the weight of the car, and other forces. But when I talked to Goodyear back at the turn of the year it said it had no control over its tyres, which is why it didn't want to continue in the land speed racing business. People build machines and don't even know themselves what aerodynamic forces they are putting through their tyres. Goodyear's view then was that it was into NASCAR racing, and that land speed racing was not part of its core business.'

Piper and Bingham insisted on taking full charge of the tyre validation programme when Visioneering became involved. They had a spin rig built to their design at Lotus Engineering in Norwich. In January and February 2006 they tried some Thompsons there which Brown had acquired early on. 'We bought four from a guy in the States, who said he'd got two brand new and two that had hardly been used,' Brown explained. 'He sent them across, Sellotaped together. I put one on a rim, inflated it to 60psi, and took it along one night to the rig. When I went back the following night it had begun to split. Part of the split was where the Sellotape had been. I took another one and the same thing happened, but a third one seemed to have been all right.'

It was a lesson that a storage and treatment protocol would be essential.

'We tried the various aircraft tyres that had been accrued,' Piper continued. 'The landing speed of a fighter is about 225mph; the first tyre we tried was heavy and deflated around that speed as it lifted off its bead seat. We were quite pleased by that because John and I had never believed in them anyway.'

Next they acquired some Goodyears from Carroll Shelby Inc in America, and free-spun them as high as 400mph without any problems. 'The free spin tests proved the Goodyears could cope,' Piper said, 'but now we had to validate them under load. The worst that could happen was that we would have to limit the car to 300mph, which is what the tyres were rated to.'

Brown added: 'We thought from discussions with Goodyear that

the growth under centrifugal force would be about an inch and a half. In actual fact it turned out to be only about four-fifths of an inch, but as your tyre grows it affects your gear ratios and it also affects the ride height of your car, so it is absolutely critical to know the effect. From our spin testing we knew what sort of gear ratios we were talking about, we knew what sort of effect on ride height the tyres were going to have. What we needed to do then was to run the tyres under load on a rig.'

Brown had found a suitable test rig at Wright Patterson Air Force Base in Dayton, Ohio, where the Space Shuttle tyres had been developed. They tested the Goodyears to 350mph under 1,700lb load there. Later they did braking running at Calspan in Buffalo, New York.

In February 2005 Bingham had to leave the project due to family problems, so Piper found an American representative called Doug Milliken to help with the tyre tests in conjunction with Brown's contact Harry Davis, a retired tyre engineer in Miami who had worked with Firestone during Art Arfons' heyday in the '60s. 'They were absolutely superb,' Piper enthused. 'Doug oversaw the tests for us, and Harry examined the tyres afterwards.'

The testing at Wright Patterson was not without its problems. Because of liability issues, Piper had to be very careful that the tests were fully regulated. 'Doug and I wrote our own tyre test standard, based on an SAE aircraft tyre standard that we had appropriated. We had to be absolutely fastidious with the procedure and have it approved by a chap called Greer at Wright Patterson. There was one great moment when I asked him to have a look at our test standard and the SAE standard. I asked him if the latter looked familiar, and he replied 'Yeah, I wrote it!' So I knew we were in safe hands.'

The Wright Patterson rig was as big as a house and comprised a solid steel wheel of 10ft diameter. It hadn't been used for 350mph testing for years. 'The bottom of the cellar it ran in had a sump full of gunge that had accumulated all that time,' Piper recalled. 'The windage of the wheel at 300mph-plus sucked all of that out and sprayed it everywhere! We lost days while they cleaned it all up. On the next test a pipe broke and the tyre deflated at 280mph. By the time they stopped the wheel it had reached 300. The tyre still held

The smaller size of the Goodyears allowed a dramatic reduction in the cross-sectional area of JCB Dieselmax, which in turn boosted its performance potential significantly.

together on the rim, so at least we had inadvertently tested its run-flat capability. Then a clip on a thermocouple wire broke, and went through the camera and laser head, but that tyre got to 310.

'It took a couple of days to prepare the rig for each test, and I was beginning to get desperate. I decided we needed to be more aggressive on the ramp-up speed for the tyres. But next time out the bearings went in the test rig and it overheated. But that tyre got to 340mph. Now we faced a week of downtime while the rig was dismantled. But because this was a US Air Force Base everything had to be done by the book. Replacement parts had to be approved, designed and put out to tender to three places. I was tearing my hair out. They were talking of a three-week delay overall.'

In desperation Piper had them email him the bearing arrangement. He received it on a Friday and had parts drawn up that afternoon. He then called on his old engineering mentor Roy Golding, an 80-year-old retiree who used to work for Cooper in F1, and he made a new hub carrier over the weekend. Piper sourced new bearings and had them installed by Monday and the new components arrived at Wright Patterson and were installed on the rig by the Tuesday. 'The Yanks were completely gobsmacked by all that!'

Eventually they ran a tyre at 350mph under 1,700lb load, and Piper decided that if it survived four cycles at that speed it could be considered validated.

'We did 335mph, 340, 345, 350 and 350 again,' he recalled. 'On the third run at 350mph the tyre started to blister on the outer edges. We figured that would be safe if they were changed at turnaround on the record runs. It gave us a safety margin. We also played with pressures. Normally we ran them at 70psi; running them at 80 spread the blisters into the centre of the tread.'

They developed a very careful handling protocol which entailed mounting the tyre and giving it a 12-hour pressure soak at 70psi. Then it got a 20-minute break-in period at 60mph, after which the tyre was allowed to cool to room temperature and then repressurised. 'Greer called that letting the molecules get to know each other, and said that the chemical change that resulted in the structure improved the tyre. That was our key difference, how we treated our tyres. Most land speed racers just store them, bolt them on and go. We treated ours like Royalty. We stored them at 30psi, flat on the rims not upright, and kept them out of hard sunlight. I used to read to them before they went to bed. All of that, from the break-in to the star treatment, was a very significant factor.'

They ran another tyre without breaking it in and it blistered on its third run and got worse on its fourth, but after it had been cut up and Davis had examined the sections under a microscope, he detected no degradation of the outer fibres.

'We thus concluded that at last we had got a tyre that would hold up at 350mph, so long as once a set had run over 340 we didn't use it again.'

The whole issue of sourcing a suitable tyre highlighted the problem facing land speed racers: because of the product liability laws there were few proprietary tyres available. 'These tyres we were buying,' Brown said, 'there's no business in them. They are $378 a copy. I suppose out of all these boys who are racing, if you sold 2,000 tyres in a season you'd make $800,000 a year. That's not a business, so unless Goodyear was going to do it for advertising, there was no base for it doing land speed tyres, unless you put them up to $5,000 a copy. But if we could have bought validated tyres for that, I think we'd have been dying to buy them!'

↑ **Chief designer John Piper insisted that the tyres be pampered; they were kept out of direct sunlight and were stored flat at all times.**

↓ **Goodyear's Eagle racing tyre was available off the shelf; JCB went to great lengths to validate it thoroughly under load to a maximum speed of 350mph.**

THE WORLD'S FASTEST DIESEL

# CHAPTER 8

# GREEN FOR GO

Back in 1994, when he was putting the ThrustSSC programme together, Richard Noble arranged for a group of potential drivers to be tested in rally cars at Chris Birkbeck's school in Brotton, near Saltburn on the north-east coast of England, under the supervision of star driver Russell Brookes. The deal was that each got four practice laps, then three hot laps. You could go off course on the practice laps, but if you did that on the three hot laps, that was the end of the road.

Mainly the contenders were RAF fighter pilots or 747 pilots. The two who stood out were RAF pilots Dick Downs and Andy Green. But where Downs would live on the ragged edge, relying totally on his car control to get himself out of trouble while hitting his stride straight away, Green had a more cerebral approach. He would work up to his speed before putting it all together in a final lap that would match Downs.

There were other tests, conducted at DERA under the auspices of Roger Green (no relation), and they, in conjunction with the rally tests, marked out Green as the clear choice.

Subsequently, the way in which he conducted himself in all the build-up to the SSC runs, both in testing on Jordan's Al Jafr Desert and later for real on the Black Rock Desert in Nevada, demonstrated why he was such a superb choice. Green was patient, flexible, quietly demanding, and knew his own mind. But more than that, he was an excellent motivator, appeared to have what had to be a sizable ego under complete control, and never lost his cool.

One night in Petra, during the Al Jafr tests, he spent the entire time on the phone to former Grand Prix driver John Miles back in the UK. Green's experience at speed on the desert that day suggested to him that SSC was never going to work well enough to challenge the record. The jetcar had unusual rear-wheel steering and all the perceived wisdom concerning it was that the driver had to make very gentle inputs so as not to excite it and thus exacerbate its fundamental instability. Green had found that day that such an approach did not work. He and Miles talked it through from every aspect, and the next day Green went out and fought

the monster in a different manner, making such rapid inputs that he effectively stayed ahead of the car and the physics all the way. Had he not been able to master the car in this manner, the ThrustSSC project would never have succeeded.

Subsequently, winding on opposite lock every time he accelerated through 620mph, because of an unusual and never fully understood aerodynamic aberration that the jetcar displayed, Green set two land speed records over 700, the second the world's only supersonic performance on land.

Noble thus had no second thoughts on a driver for Project H1. When Tim Leverton approached Green in March 2005, he remembered: 'I had dinner with Andy, whom Richard had suggested might like to drive. He seemed very keen.'

The approach, like the rest of the project, was made with great secrecy. 'I thought at the time that Tim was Andy's other woman!' joked Green's girlfriend Sophy Gardner, herself an RAF high flier.

Born in Atherstone, Warwickshire, Green won an RAF Scholarship to Oxford, where he graduated with First Class Honours in Maths and excelled in College and University rowing and flying. He then served full time with the RAF undertaking flying training before being selected to fly Phantoms. He spent five years on the 'mighty F4' before moving on to a two-year stint flying Tornados. That brought him to Farnborough and thence to the ThrustSSC programme.

Subsequently he did another Tornado F3 tour as a Flight Commander, one year at staff college in Australia, and was then promoted to Wing Commander and spent two years in the Permanent Joint HQ at Northwood running ops in Afghanistan and Iraq. By March 2005 he was OC Operations Wing at RAF Wittering, running the airfield and all other Station operations at the 'Home of the Harrier', while also acting as Deputy Station Commander. It was typical of his character that he described his other activities thus: 'Usual stupid pastime stuff: now captain of the RAF Cresta team, flying a Pitts Special at weekends, skydiving with Sophy, skipper for sailing holidays, plus another record...'

'I had to think about Tim's offer for nearly two seconds before I

Andy Green: **Mr Supersonic, the holder of two world land speed records, and Bonneville aficionado.**

**A trained RAF pilot with a First in Maths from Oxford, Green was always lucid when explaining technical points in presentations.**

**Green poses with ThrustSSC, in which he became the only man ever to break through the sound barrier on land.**

agreed to have a chat with him,' he said. 'It's not just a showcase for JCB, its about showing how good British engineering is. The whole package – the Ricardo-developed JCB engines and the Visioneering chassis – is a fantastic product and we are going to go to the world-famous Bonneville Speed Week to show not just the Americans but the whole world just how good British engineering is.'

The Bonneville thing was crucial. Back in the late '90s Green was due to drive an MG record car at Bonneville, but the programme ultimately foundered. He was a regular visitor to Speed Week and, secretly, felt that part of his make-up as a record breaker would always be missing until he had vindicated himself on the hallowed salt.

'We will be following in the straightline racing tradition of Sir Malcolm Campbell, George Eyston and John Cobb, three of the greats of record breaking,' he said. 'And we will be running at the sport's spiritual home, the remarkable Bonneville Salt Flats.

'We are building a British car, with British engines, and taking it to America to set a spectacular diesel automobile record. How could anyone not find that exciting?

'Diesel engineering has a great future as more and more motorists choose the diesel option, and I am delighted to be part of an engineering project that will contribute a great deal more knowledge to that important cause. I am really looking forward to seeing another British entry in the "300mph Club", and a diesel-engined, wheel-driven one at that.'

He had reservations, however. 'I was a little concerned that a large corporate team might take an arrogant, know-it-all approach to this sport, trying to "buy" a record while ignoring those who really live and breathe it. I could not have been more wrong – every one of them, right from Tim Leverton to Annie Berrisford, all got this sport right away – they all got a bad case of "salt fever"!'

Leverton accepted right from the start that driving skill would be a crucial part of the programme, and never subscribed to the popular view that all a record breaker has to do is hold the wheel for the sake of appearances while keeping his right foot buried to the floor. That is as naïve and inaccurate as the idea that all Grand Prix drivers are well behaved gentlemen on the track and saints off it.

'Driving skill counts for a great deal,' Leverton acknowledged. 'You

'One of the issues we felt very early on is that we had to have somebody who was very cool and professional, a qualified person to drive, not a celebrity racing driver type of person. The thing about Andy Green is that he is a very rational kind of individual capable of dealing with a very high cockpit workrate. And because he

have to know how to react. It's not the same as running round a closed circuit or on tarmac. It's about feeling the grip, of knowing what to do. You are very dependent on the conditions and you cannot control that.

'In terms of the perfect car, the main challenge, once you have done the physics and know you have enough power and got the basic parameters in place, is to make a driveable car.

'One of the issues we felt very early on is that we had to have somebody who was very cool and professional, a qualified person to drive, not a celebrity racing driver type of person. The thing about Andy Green is that he is a very rational kind of individual capable of dealing with a very high cockpit work rate. And because he drove ThrustSSC he was very qualified. Although this was half the speed, it was still plenty fast enough to be very interesting. It's

not going to be like an F1 car with bags of downforce. It's going to be far livelier in some respects. Andy is also going to have to feel the car and the interaction between tyre contact patch and salt with greater sensitivity than an F1 driver might as downforce squashes his tyres into the road. He is always going to be juggling the throttle to maintain forward velocity and momentum, while maximising all-important traction.'

What the JCB team perhaps didn't realise at the outset was that they would be buying in much more than Green's fundamental skill at the wheel. Part of the package was a willingness to get into even the smallest details – things such as instrument panel design or the strength calculations on the parachute strops – as he enthusiastically applied an intelligence the depth of which at times was hugely impressive.

Prior to the driving side of Project H1, Green was not too proud to go away and train for his new mission. He took himself off to former Grand Prix driver Jonathan Palmer's facility at Bedford Autodrome for a brush-up course in car control.

'The training at Bedford was my initiative, to improve my car handling skills and "feel". I found the training that I had done at Silverstone 10 years ago proved to be surprisingly useful when SSC started making some of its larger off-axis excursions. The way I explained it to the superb guys at Bedford – Phil Gough and Nicky Faulkner – the aim was for me to recognise when I was inside the control limit/at the control limit/over the limit (ie not fully in control). If over the limit, then knowing why and being able to select and apply the appropriate corrective response, and not just panic and overreact instead. A lot of straightline driving is psychological rather than physical (true of all racing, I know, but a unique balance in this sport). Put it another way, driving in a straight line is generally not that difficult (although SSC transonic

was an exception!), but screwing it up is really easy (witness the number of cars at Bonneville that spin out at high speed). The aim at Bedford was to develop my feel for the control limit(s), refine my physical responses and prepare my mind to apply them calmly and precisely at high speed and under high stress. Easy, really!

'I had three great track sessions, using their Nissan 350Zs, Palmer Audi single-seaters, and the Palmer Jaguar two-seater – and the full range of speeds, which gave me a great chance to work through the control limits time and again while experimenting with wheel-driven handling in lots of different ways. I could tell that the Bedford training was working when, driving home afterwards in the wet, one of my road car's wheels slipped very slightly on a white line on a roundabout. I didn't even have to think about it – I knew not only that it was a rear, but could feel (rather than work out) which one. Subsequently, knowing what was happening at both ends of the Dieselmax gave me a lot of confidence at the higher speeds and allowed me to press harder than would otherwise have been comfortable.

'Subsequently I had a discussion about this training aims with the American writer "Landspeed" Louise Noeth, who was initially adamant that it was too "professional" and high-budget for other teams. I pointed out that tens of thousands of dollars and thousands of hours of work can all be thrown away for the want of skills learned in a few hundred dollars' worth of track-day training. She eventually came round to the idea that focussing solely on the car for Bonneville, and ignoring the driver, might after all be a little unbalanced... I just hope she doesn't go round bollocking every team out there "because Andy Green said so"!'

Green also did training of another sort, preparing himself for everything he could expect at Bonneville. 'I had a lot of hot baths over July and early August, as I did before the SSC desert campaigns. It is a really good way to acclimatise quickly and was a tip given to me by the late Roger Green who was so closely involved with the Farnborough driver selection for SSC.'

From the moment he sat in ThrustSSC, Andy Green raised the ante for the speed record seeker to the sort of level that Ayrton Senna and Michael Schumacher did in Grand Prix driving. There was simply no better driver for JCB Dieselmax.

Andy Green and his big yellow banana: there was nobody cooler for the job, as he would prove conclusively at Bonneville.

From the moment he sat in ThrustSSC, Andy Green raised the ante for the speed record seeker to the sort of level that Ayrton Senna and Michael Schumacher brought to grand prix driving. There was simply no better driver for JCB Dieselmax.

# CHAPTER 9

# FIRST STEPS

In July 2006 JCB Dieselmax was finally ready for rollout and its first test runs. These would be conducted on the north taxiway at RAF Wittering near Peterborough, the 'Home of the Harrier' airbase at which Andy Green was a Wing Commander.

The car arrived there in the early hours of Tuesday the 18th. The project was around ten days behind the schedule mapped out back in October 2005, and now they had just 23 days before the start of Bonneville Speed Week. Each day thus had to be a step forward if they were going to meet the challenge ahead. But there were further delays. The 'to do' list was too long, so it was decided to carry out all of the work and delay running the car until Friday the 21st.

'For whatever reason we only ended up with the drivelines in the car about four weeks ago,' Tim Leverton explained, 'so basically we missed the date of 5 July which was the target to be here at Wittering.

'The engines were started for the first time last weekend. The rear engine was fired up at 2.30 on Sunday morning the 16th, and we attempted to start the front that afternoon but there was a fuel rail leak. We also had a failure of an oil cooler on the rear engine which meant that we got water into the oil circuit, so we had to stop to work on that.

'We had actually reached a point where we had effectively got the car ready to put fluids in and ready to start, but a lot of time was lost then trying to start the engines, which should have been used to finish the car.

'Over the weekend John (Piper) and I independently came to the same conclusion: that we had to move the car, to try and recover lost time. It arrived at Wittering at 2.30 Tuesday morning. In the process of handling it for the first time it fell off one of the jacks and was damaged. Not seriously, but enough to create a to-do list of repair work for Tuesday morning. That was when the whole team got together for the first time.'

Pulling together people from disparate walks of life and forging them into a cohesive team takes time, but JCB had a head start.

On the day of the press launch back on 20 April, the whole team had met for the first time in one place at JCB's Rocester HQ. During their meeting Richard Noble had spoken about the nature of the challenge a team faces in breaking a world record. The day after, reflecting on that meeting, both Leverton and Noble were concerned about how little time was available to build up an understanding between the three company groups of what was now the JCB Dieselmax team. Noble recommended some team building.

Leverton turned to Humphrey Walters to design a team-building process for the entire Dieselmax team – those who would be going to Utah as well as those remaining behind in the UK to support. Walters had worked as teamworking coach alongside Sir Clive Woodward for six years with the World Cup-winning English rugby team, and in December 2005 had been the guest speaker at JCB's Annual Awards event, where JCB people are recognised for outstanding achievement.

The team-building event took place in Coventry in the last week of May. Some of the results of this event were published as notes in a gift Filofax, each member's personal revelations providing a curiously moving insight into their secret motivations.

Leverton acknowledged the contribution the team-building had made to a fast start at Wittering: 'That was a good investment, to have everybody together. I was a little bit sceptical. I thought it was a bit late. But it was very good. Those things in the Filofax were written by a partner, dictated to them by the various individuals, so it was quite a thing to open up and share them. All of it meant that by the time they got to Wittering, everyone had already met each other. They'd already got through the polite "who are yous?"

'Richard had spoken to us in April about the record-breaking spirit, and about what it takes, and we did the thing with Humphrey, but we had received Richard's message and thought, "Yeah, but we are professionals." You know what I mean? But the moment we all got together at Wittering, and got the yellow shirts on, we weren't just professionals any more, we were a team who had skills, and the barriers dropped.'

Friday morning, the 21st, brought an oil leak on the front engine, and low oil pressure and some water in the oil on the rear. It also

John Piper and Andy Green confer at RAF Wittering before Green tries to select all six gears in each transmission, with both engines running.

'John and I independently came to the same conclusion:
that we had to move the car, to try and recover lost time.'

**Tim Leverton**

Minus wheels and tyres, and bodywork, JCB Dieselmax is unloaded at RAF Wittering on July 18th 2006.

provided an insight for visitors into the sheer complexity of a car that had two engines, two transmissions, and a raft of complex electronics to help systems talk to one another. Just getting both engines fired, then selecting gears individually, then doing so in synchronisation, was a painstaking task that required fearsome intelligence and patience from the engineers.

'We've selected gears for the first time without an adult present,' quipped a smiling Alastair Macqueen as all six worked, in harmony, each end of the car.

The work was carried out with the calmness of professionals who knew their job. The Dieselmax team might be young, but already it was melding together as more than 20 people worked 12-hour days, moving busily around the streamliner which sat in the middle of its awning like some giant metal cadaver awaiting an autopsy. John Piper watched over everything like a doting father, whatever emotions he was feeling masked by a preternaturally calm exterior.

Even naked, JCB Dieselmax was a thing of breathtaking beauty that seduced you with its engineering. There were nice touches everywhere, the neatest perhaps being the engraved JCB logos on the aluminium top frames that strengthened each engine bay. They had been machined by Visioneering from solid billets. 'I said to John, "You won't want the same standard of finish on the underside of the frames, will you?"' revealed company boss Brian Horner, 'and he immediately replied, "Oh yes!"'

Green arrived that morning, smart in his RAF uniform and Thunderbirds cap, all usual loping gait, habitual smile and friendly greeting. Later he sat in the cockpit, surrounded by a phalanx of computers.

'We have an open communications system,' he explained, having pushed it through. 'It needs radio discipline but I want everyone to know and be part of the loop. I'm not out doing laps for hours, just a few minutes of runs at a time, and they should all be part of it. An information hierarchy is a hangover from F1 and I don't want that. Information flow can be a control, and it shouldn't be like that.'

The engines ran for the longest they had so far while installed in the car – 19 minutes; but by 19.25 a gearbox sensor problem was preventing the front engine from engaging gears. By 21.50, with darkness stealing over the airfield, they stood down until Saturday.

The following morning the car was ready again, the sensor problem solved. It was sunny to begin with, but it rained mid-morning, quite heavily, before drying out again. 'There's a rainbow out there somewhere,' Piper said, pointing down the end of the chosen runway.

At 13.15 there was a sudden exodus of personnel from the awning and Dieselmax was pushed out on to the runway, tension mounting. Green looked businesslike in his bright yellow overalls and the Arai helmet that had been professionally liveried in JCB colours and RAF logos by Mike Fairholme.

The start-up procedure was always the same. The engines had to be pre-heated, so two trolley-mounted water heaters were used to bring the coolant to around 85°C. Once they had reached that there was a 'pre-flight' checklist comprising a whole series of systems checks, such as tyres, parachutes, gauges, radio etc. Race engineer Alastair Macqueen would be responsible for running the car on the salt, and for going through the checklist. John Piper would then have overall responsibility for clearing the car to run.

Green did not have to start the engines himself. A technician did that via a remote battery pack connected to generators in the support trailers. Matt Beasley had overall responsibility for the engines.

The streamliner faced days of preparation under its awning before it was finally ready for its maiden run.

Finalised dashboard and switch layout.

Once they had been started the crew loaded the ice tank. The body panels were then fitted and the cockpit canopy was lowered. Piper gave Colin Bond the okay for the push-start.

On this occasion the decision had been taken not to run with the distinctive yellow bodywork, nor with the rear fin. Thus it was the naked version of JCB Dieselmax that was finally lined up on the north taxiway just before 2.30 in the afternoon. It was quite warm but muggy, with the hint of a storm in the offing. Wittering offered 9,000ft of runway, up to 3,000 of which would be used for acceleration.

At 14.40, Dieselmax's first powered run finally began. Bond in the Fastrac carefully pushed it up to 40mph, dwarfing it in the process in a mechanical dance of midget and monster, before Green activated the steering-wheel paddle-shift to select first gear and accelerated away in a cloud of smoke that, Matt Beasley patiently explained, was due to unburnt fuel in the system that could only be cleared out once the engines came under load.

Unusually, Green admitted to slight trepidation. 'Just before Colin gave me the push I felt a frisson of nervousness,' he said. 'This is a huge team effort until I run the car, and from then on you are on your own. I said to myself, "Don't mess this up!" But as soon as I felt Colin pushing me and Dieselmax was rolling I had something to focus on and things went back to normal.'

He only reached 61mph before he got the message over the radio to shut down: 'You're losing lots of coolant, major call on the coolant.' He pulled up halfway down the course and was towed back. Inspection subsequently revealed it was a false alarm; it was just overflow from the undertray following some leakage earlier on when there had been an initial delay when the electronics had shut down the systems.

It was inauspicious for a maiden run, but Green was happy. 'This showed how well the car has been put together,' he said. 'To be honest, it felt bloody awful just idling because the level of vibration felt terrific at 1,900rpm, but once it got going it felt really smooth and even on a light throttle it already felt very quick.'

Piper had a different summation of that first run. 'It's like passing a kidney stone,' he said. 'You know you've got to do it and it really hurts, but once you have it's the most wonderful relief!'

They hoped to get a full pass run in that day, but looking at the darkening sky Macqueen said: 'Okay guys, we're gonna get wet. I think we need to put the car back in the hangar...' They had literally just done so when the heavens opened. And as Leverton gave everyone a pep talk speech in the canteen tent, there was a banshee wail from the growing wind outside and various bits of equipment started to head off to Peterborough. It was a great bit of theatre, until the endless torrent of rain threatened to flood everything. It was as if Mother Nature was giving them as many lessons in record breaking as she could squeeze into one day.

'Seeing the car run for the very first was a special moment for the whole team,' Leverton said. 'The thrill was when Andy put it in gear and accelerated hard. This is the real start of our testing, which is a critical part of the record attempt.'

One of the few problems arose when, seeking to warm the engines up quicker, Green did a 'lap' comprising two runways. There was insufficient clearance between a rear tyre and one of the carbon-fibre streamlining spats, and as he put side load into the tyre the bodywork sliced through the sidewall. But otherwise, for a new and highly complex car whose systems required continual monitoring, the streamliner performed with remarkable reliability.

**Fastrac dwarfs Dieselmax as Colin Bond pushes Green at the start of the run, before the streamliner gathers pace under its own power.**

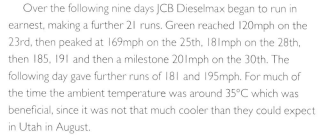

Subsequent runs were made with full bodywork fitted, and using the parachute brake.

Not all of them went smoothly, but testing never does.

Over the following nine days JCB Dieselmax began to run in earnest, making a further 21 runs. Green reached 120mph on the 23rd, then peaked at 169mph on the 25th, 181mph on the 28th, then 185, 191 and then a milestone 201mph on the 30th. The following day gave further runs of 181 and 195mph. For much of the time the ambient temperature was around 35°C which was beneficial, since it was not that much cooler than they could expect in Utah in August.

'We're content with the way things went today,' Green said after the runs on the 30th. 'The weather was ideal and, apart from a half-hour hold-up when we changed electronic sensors after the trial run, it all went well. I'm so impressed with what has been achieved. Exceeding a peak speed of 200mph really shows the potential of the car to break the record. Combined, the engines have twice the power of a Formula One car and it's remarkably easy to drive. It steers very well, the brakes work smoothly, and the chassis is extremely stiff. That gives you the confidence you need when accelerating to very high speeds and then coming to a stop in a limited space.

'We've been working to an exceptionally tight timescale and we're having to learn new things every day, from engine and transmission performance to parachute deployment,' he continued. 'It's impossible for everything to work perfectly when testing land speed record vehicles as you're pushing the boundaries, but we're on target.'

Leverton, too, was very pleased with progress. 'We have learnt a huge amount about the car and the team has done a fantastic job of overcoming the many challenges we have inevitably faced in such a complex and demanding project. I am really proud that we have exceeded 200mph at this stage of development, and now we can be more confident about achieving our target of 300mph at Bonneville.'

In reaching 201mph, Green hadn't got out of third gear or exceeded 3,300rpm. From initial chaos had come order.

'There was even a point on the 30th when we fitted three runs into an hour and a half, and on each one the car progressively became easier to drive,' Leverton noted. 'It reached its performance very much more quickly, which in the confined length of the 9,000ft runway, was helpful. We were using 2,500 to 3,000ft to clear the engines when they were cold. We came up with the warm-up

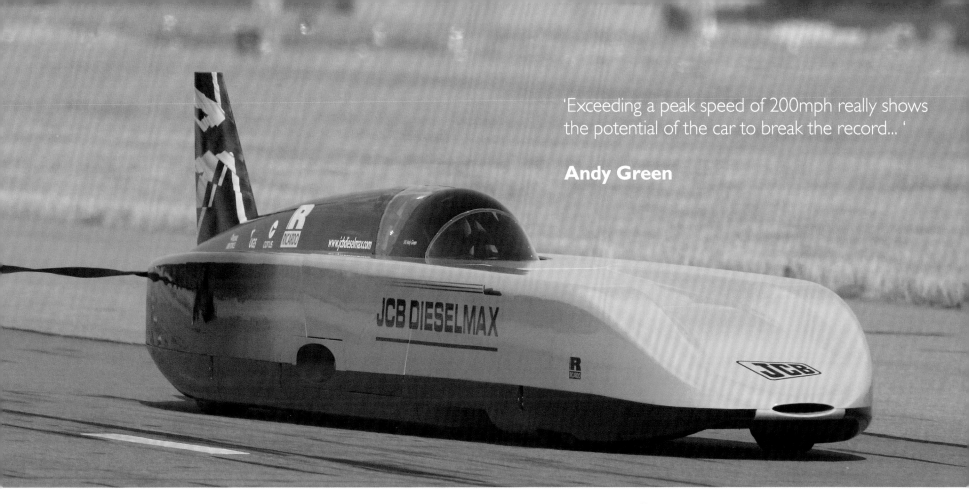

'Exceeding a peak speed of 200mph really shows the potential of the car to break the record... '

**Andy Green**

procedure which didn't work quite as we expected the first time, and led to the tyre failure, but on the Sunday we did seven runs, in two batches, and on the second to last run we did 201mph, momentarily, at the end of the runway.'

In 10 days at Wittering they had pulled the project back on schedule, and met all the objectives they had for the test. There was a lengthy list of more than 100 criteria that had to be validated. 'We had a traffic light system,' Leverton explained, 'green, amber, red. We had no reds and only a few ambers. We even started to do some preparation work for Bonneville, but there was limited time.' The team removed the ice tank and the rear fin, and the car was strapped on to a pallet and loaded on to a 747 cargo plane. Along with 25 tonnes of equipment , it was then shipped over to Salt Lake City, where it arrived on the Sunday night, the 6th of August.'

They had packed six weeks' work into the fortnight. It had been gruelling, without any let-up in the pressure, but now they were back on schedule. They were ready for the real challenge to begin.

After peaking at 201mph in only 9,000ft, a delighted Green confers with John Piper.

# CHAPTER 10

# THE SPECTRE OF FAILURE

The JCB Dieselmax team set up camp in an old hangar out at Wendover Airfield, far from the opulence of Salt Lake City. The place had history. Just down the road was Atomic Hangar 1831 that Colonel Paul Tibbetts and the 393rd Bombardment Squadron of the 509th Composite Group had utilised for operations and maintenance as they practiced for the mission that would become the historic *Enola Gay* flight to bomb Hiroshima. Later, in the hangar JCB now occupied, Donald Campbell and Richard Noble would take refuge during their respective 1960 and 1981 attempts on the land speed record. Andy Green had less than happy memories of it from MG's stillborn record efforts in the late '90s. And Honda had used it only recently, while attacking the record for a Formula One car. A discarded wing from Alan van der Merwe's Lucky Strike BAR Honda still lay forlornly in one room where, at least one team member was convinced, they had heard the ominous warning of a rattlesnake.

The team now faced its greatest challenge. Many members had been under massive pressure for 18 months, with the planning, design and build processes, and it had never let up with the deadlines at RAF Wittering. The fact that they had hit all of their targets was a minor miracle. But the salt inspired everyone. It was an adrenaline rush, being there, seeing the place (in many cases) for the first time.

Apart from the condition of the salt, and Wendover itself which has become far more glitzy as it shamelessly chased the gambling dollar, nothing has changed at the flats since legendary speedking Sir Malcolm Campbell ventured there in 1935. The Silver Island Mountains skirt them to the north-west, the ridges still clearly visible where prehistoric Lake Lahontan once found its level. And Floating Mountain still appears to hover at the far, north-eastern, end of the course. This is one of the most unusual places on earth, and one of the few where man can achieve unlimited velocity.

The flats were named after explorer Captain B.L.E. Bonneville, and stretch for 30,000 acres close to the Utah/Nevada border. Today they are an easy, if tedious, 120-mile drive west on Interstate 80 from Salt Lake City, but they were once infamous as the place where the fated Donner-Reed migrant party, seeking a shortcut to California in 1846, suffered privations that forced them to resort to cannibalism.

Promoter W.D. Rishel was the first man to appreciate the salt flats' potential while scouting a cycle race course from New York to San Francisco in 1896, but they achieved international fame in the '30s through the efforts of Salt Lake City endurance record-setter 'Ab' Jenkins and his Mormon Meteor. Tales of the firmness of the surface attracted Campbell, who on 3 September 1935 became the first man to top 300mph with a speed of 301.129mph in his Bluebird. He was succeeded later that decade by fellow Britons Captain George Eyston in his Thunderbolt and John Cobb in his Railton Special. Until 1982, with the exception of Donald Campbell who went to Australia's Lake Eyre after his crash at Bonneville with Bluebird in 1960, the Bonneville Salt Flats were the choice of all record seekers. In an explosive duel of speed with American Art Arfons in the mid-'60s, fellow countryman Craig Breedlove became the first man to break the 400, 500 and 600mph barriers there. In 1970 American Gary Gabelich went faster still in his rocket-powered Blue Flame.

In 1981 poor weather closed down Richard Noble's first attempt on Gabelich's record with his pure-jet Thrust2, and even before he went back there in 1982 flooding at the flats forced him into his historic relocation to the Black Rock Desert in Nevada. That has now become Mecca for pure-thrust cars running on solid aluminium wheels, but after Nolan White found that the desert's sandy playa surface was unsuitable for wheel-driven cars following test runs there with his Spirit of Autopower streamliner in 1983, Bonneville remained the ideal venue on which to challenge for wheel-driven honours.

The flats usually flood in November, and it takes until around June for them to dry out again. As the water slowly evaporates, the smoothing action of the wind creates a flat, hard and level surface comprising potassium, magnesium lithium and sodium chloride (better known as ordinary table salt). As it dries further pressure ridges can develop, creating a buckling effect and these must be

**Bonneville Speed Week used two courses – JCB Dieselmax naturally needed the longer one.**

Looking east, from the Nevada side, Wendover's colourful attributes are laid out, watched over by famous cowboy Wendover Will.

Resourceful as ever, Jules Tipler and Peter Panarisi from Fingal found the way to work while topping up their tans.

smoothed away before high speeds are feasible. This is a relatively simple but painstaking task that entails dragging the course with a length of heavy railway track.

One of the greatest challenges of record breaking is to achieve perfect conditions. And that is down to pure luck. A team can research, test and develop a high-speed automobile to the nth degree, but success ultimately remains totally dependent on the prevailing weather and course conditions. Mother Nature holds all the high cards, but she smiled benignly on the JCB team.

In July 2006, when American speedking Russ Wicks had set a new 222mph record for world stockcars, Bonneville Nationals Inc president Mike Cook had praised the condition of the salt: 'It's the best I've seen it for at least 10 years. Maybe even 20.'

Ray Kelsey, of the Bureau of Land Management, explained: 'We had a wet spring and a high water table last year, which is why the track was so bumpy and never really dried out then. But this year we had a normal spring with a good amount of freshwater falling on the flats. It then gradually warmed up and dried out. Then we had a big storm come through on Memorial Day weekend (at the end of May) and that flooded it again. This time it dried slowly again and that left the surface just perfect. It's my observation that this year we just had the ideal climatic conditions.'

Speed Week was the first of three speed events that Bonneville hosts each year, and is run jointly by the SCTA and BNI. This year it fell on August 12–18.

There was a buzz for the JCB team from knowing that they had built a great car in a timescale that shocked all of the experienced racers. It was something to be proud of.

The last time the Americans had seen such a well-funded British project on the flats was back in 1960, when Donald Campbell turned up with his Bluebird CN7 to face Athol Graham, Mickey Thompson, Art Arfons and Dr Nathan Ostich. All of them had 400mph in their sights.

JCB Dieselmax immediately drew gasps of admiration, but the record number of entries for Speed Week – 499 machines had turned up – and the broad range of technical ingenuity that was on display, had the British reciprocating.

The opulence of Campbell's programme turned some Americans against it, but his detractors overlooked that he was 6,000 miles from home and thus needed copious spares. JCB Dieselmax was without question the best financed British programme since then, and most of the hot-rodders were impecunious fellows who could only afford this one shot at their goals during their season, but through a combination of honesty, openness, humility and general bonhomie the new breed of Brits were welcomed with open arms.

Team member Eoin Corrigan had worked for TWR on the Nissan Le Mans programme, for Toyota Team Europe, and then for Arrows in F1. He was happy now to be farming in his native Ireland while doing the odd bit of freelance work for Toyota's F1 programme. He'd seen enough racing for a lifetime, but found his interest quickened by what he saw at Speed Week.

'Look at what you have here,' he enthused. 'Jack Costella's Nebulous Theorem II is powered by a motorcycle engine, and has just done 358mph. It's fantastic, all the ingenuity. And the people are wonderful. The first morning, when we were down at the start for five or six hours, we had guys bringing us water and hot dogs for lunch. And that's other competitors! It really has refreshed me, being here.'

It was not all one-sided. Corrigan brought his fabricating skills

The base camp hangar at Wendover Airfield may not have been the most salubrious building, but it was steeped in record breaking history.

Key figures in the project (left to right): Ron Jones, Engine Build Technician; Ron Ayers, Aerodynamicist; Dave Haggas, Bodywork Composite Specialist; and Brian Horner, Chief Executive, Visioneering.

Surrounded by all the myriad spares necessary for such a complex endeavour 6000 miles from home, JCB Dieselmax continues to command attention.

**Chris Dee had one of the most crucial roles: looking after the tyres.**

to bear on behalf of several competitors, two of whom went on to break records. Ayers, in his inimitable diffident manner, offered his aerodynamic advice freely to two motorcycle teams and one car racer, and was fascinated by the University of Iowa's Buckeye Bullet streamliner and the proposal to run it with power via a fuel cell. The quiet statesman of record breaking was happy to spend time talking with anyone and everyone about the nuances of the game.

John Piper was approached one morning by a Californian engineer who begged him for the drawings for Dieselmax's parachute release mechanism so that he could put it into production. He offered Visioneering a cut of the profits, and was stunned when Piper nonchalantly told him he could have the drawings for nothing.

Subsequently, Colin Bond would use the various JCB machines that accompanied Dieselmax to the salt – a Loadall telescopic handler and a backhoe – to clear heavy, semi-submerged debris, such as telegraph poles, from the south western end of the course. Even something as small as the submerged rim of a 55 gallon oil barrel had been sufficient to trip Tom Burkland's 450mph Burkland streamliner into a series of 70mph rolls that all but destroyed it, when he ran into rough salt after a very high-speed pass back in 2001. The resultant damage required a total rebuild that kept the racing family team out of business until 2004.

These seemingly small acts were received with gratitude by the people who return to the salt again and again. The integration of the two apparently disparate philosophies was seamless and unforced.

'The whole team felt it was a privilege to be part of the famous Bonneville Speed Week,' Green said subsequently, 'and recognised that they had a responsibility to contribute to the magical sport of straightline racing, Bonneville style. The Dieselmax team did Speed Week superbly, with the likes of aerodynamicist Ron, "Mr Fixit" Duffy Sheardown, Eoin and anyone else with time to spare spending hours hosting our constant stream of visitors. All of the JCB, Ricardo and Visioneering personnel have every reason to be very proud of themselves: they were remarkable as a team and, I think, are just the sort of people who deserve to be part of the Bonneville legend.

'We had a fantastic level of support from everyone out there. It was a great feeling to talk to all of the other teams at Speed Week, none of whom begrudged us the JCB budget and all of whom wished us the very best of luck – I can't think of another form of motorsport where people are so generous.'

Even in Wendover, the closest town that lies within ten miles of the salt, the British found the same spirit that the Thrust2 and ThrustSSC teams had enjoyed from the people of Gerlach, 120 miles north of Reno up by the Black Rock Desert. There were plenty of late-night watering holes in town: the bars of the gaudy gambling casino hotels such as the Wendover Nugget, the Montego Bay, the Peppermill and the Rainbow, but most people also dropped into Carmen's Black and White, a small bar that was so similar to Bev's Miners' Club in Gerlach. It was a quiet place much of the time, run by Carmen and Shawna, and besides quenching their thirst Carmen also volunteered to do all of the team's laundry for the duration.

Dieselmax had already partly been scrutineered as Lee Kennedy travelled over to have an official look at Wittering, and at 06.15 on the morning of Saturday, 12 August, the process was completed in the hangar. By 10.00 the car stood in line ready for the long course to open at midday.

It was always clear that Speed Week would impose less than optimal conditions on running Dieselmax, but it was a crucial part of the development programme. The ideal time to run a fast car is in the relative cool of the morning before the sun draws moisture to the surface and makes the course more slippery, and when the effect of altitude is minimised. It is also the time when the wind is most likely to be minimal. The procedure there calls for competitors to line up awaiting a start. It can be long and convoluted, but it's completely fair. On this occasion it meant that Dieselmax sat for six hours before its slot came up.

This presented special problems. The engine pre-heaters and computers all had to be moved every time the car gained another space in the line-up. But the team adapted well, and at 16.00 hrs JCB Dieselmax finally made its first run on the salt. Ironically, since Green had never driven at Bonneville he had to be regarded as a rookie, his two 700+ mph land speed records

'The Dieselmax team did Speed Week superbly, with the likes of aerodynamicist Ron, 'Mr Fixit' Duffy Sheardown, Eoin and anyone else with time to spare spending hours hosting our constant stream of visitors. All of the JCB, Ricardo and Visioneering personnel have every reason to be very proud of themselves: they were remarkable as a team and, I think, are just the sort of people who deserve to be part of the Bonneville legend.'

**Andy Green**

and unique supersonic status notwithstanding.

'Watching Dieselmax set off down the "long course" to complete its first ever run on the salt brought a lump to my throat, I can tell you!' Leverton confessed.

Green got away after the usual push start procedure worked well (even though it was Colin Bond's first go on the salt too), and recorded a peak speed of 163mph. This was respectable enough for Mike Cook to agree that Andy could forego further orientation and get his rookie signature there and then. New cars are also regarded as rookies at Bonneville, and JCB Dieselmax was likewise cleared.

Beasley noted that only the front engine was running on boost, however. Green made an agreed three attempts to initiate boost on the rear engine, before deploying his braking parachute and pulling off course at the three mile point.

This was all in keeping with a rookie orientation run, so the outside world did not realise there was a problem. And on the positive side Green reported that the car handled well,

**The JCB** team was welcoming and appreciative of American interest, as visitors flocked to see the best-looking car on the salt.

**Green** (far left) was always in demand but never lost his cool as media clamoured for his attention.

particularly in the traction and braking departments, and subsequent inspection with the bodywork removed indicated little ingress of salt into either the engine bays or the wheelarches.

During the inspection it was also discovered that the rear diesel particulate filter had disintegrated, possibly due to excessive exhaust backpressure, so there was hope that the boost problem had already been identified. That, however, would prove to be optimistic.

Besides its dual engines and transmissions and four-wheel drive, Dieselmax had enough computerised control units to run a small country. Getting all of them to talk the same language to each other was a major challenge. Relentless work, patience and the inherent excellence of the engineering had paid off during the 22 runs at Wittering, but at Bonneville fresh issues arose. In further preliminary runs, eight of them back at the airfield, the multi-million pound car continually flopped. The front engine would reach optimum working temperature and sustain turbo boost; the rear would not. It went along for the ride, acting like a brake.

With a driver of Green's calibre the man at the wheel could be eliminated in the search for an answer. He remained his usual analytical self, working through all the cockpit protocols to try and bring the rear engine into play. On the one occasion he did, however, the front engine took a break in protest.

In an attempt to sort the problem six runs were made at Wendover Airfield early on the 15th. The fuel supply to the front engine was leaned off in first gear only, and they were able to establish full boost on the rear engine in first gear and boost on both engines in second. The car was taken back to the salt, but high crosswinds delayed the start until 10.30 and backed up the queue. Dieselmax was the penultimate car to run and this time the rear engine went on to boost in first gear as planned, but as soon as Green hit second the front engine refused to pick up. The peak speed was 186mph.

Once again they retreated to Wendover Airfield, where Beasley came up with the idea of using a balance pipe as a mechanical link between the two engines that would ensure the available boost was distributed evenly.

There was a further kick that day when news filtered through that they had been beaten to the 300mph mark for diesels. For five years 63-year-old veteran Roy Lewis had been bringing his intriguing Chassis Engineering Special to the salt, in search of the record. He had built it with his business partner, and the pencil-slim machine was almost 30ft long but no wider than 28in. It was powered by a heavily modified turbocharged 5.9 litre Cummins 6BTA six-cylinder diesel engine.

This was Lewis's day, as he backed a run of 303mph with a 309mph return to cement a new SCTA-BNI national record of 306.8mph.

'We had a couple of real good runs, and I believe the car is capable of more,' he said as he celebrated the triumph for which he had worked so diligently.

In the JCB camp there was nothing but praise for a job well done. The success was not troubling from an engineering point of view, because JCB Dieselmax clearly had more than sufficient potential to exceed that speed.

Subsequently there was a nice moment on the salt when both cars and drivers were captured together for posterity. 'We're gonna have to hurry up, you've got three minutes,' Green said with uncharacteristic acerbity to project photographer Andy Ferraro, who managed the job in less than that. Typically, Green later apologised for hassling him, but it was another little sign of the underlying tension and determination to get going and find a cure, after the first run on 17 August had been another failure.

As Leverton said, they were looking down a barrel at the most embarrassing catastrophe.

The spectre of failure sat on the project's shoulder. If JCB Dieselmax's boost problems persisted and if, by some perverse fate, it turned out that they could not be fixed and the team had to return to the UK without a record of its own, the world would remember only that the little guys had upstaged the big guys.

**Anglo American racers: Roy Lewis and Andy Green pose with their Chassis Engineering Special and JCB Dieselmax, just before Green prepared to challenge the Bonneville veteran's hard-won record.**

# CHAPTER II

# BREAKING THROUGH

The reason for Andy Green's terseness on Thursday 17 August was plain for all to see. After a long wait on the salt the previous day the long course had been closed due to 25mph crosswinds. Further test runs at the airfield had indicated that the engine boost problem had been solved, but the first run that Thursday had been another disaster. It was the slowest yet, and after all the hope induced by the airfield runs that they had sorted things out, the balance pipe did not appear to make any difference on the salt no matter what Green tried in the cockpit.

A thoroughly disillusioned team of engineers – including Tim Leverton, Dave Brown, Matt Beasley, Jon Oakey, John Piper, Alastair Macqueen, Brian Horner, Ron Ayers and Richard Noble – sat glumly in the air-conditioned JCB special events trailer, desperately trying to figure out why the car would behave itself on tarmac at the airfield, and misbehave the minute it got salt under its wheels. You could cut the tension with a knife.

They had formulated their plan of action to encourage the rear engine to do its work, and had put it into effect the previous day as Green ran up and down the airfield back in Wendover. Essentially, each engine needed an exhaust temperature in excess of 400°C before boost could be sustained. One of the potential cures was to fit the boost balance pipe between the two engines. Another was for Green initially to feather the brakes with his left foot to give the engines something to work against after Bond and observer Neil Smith had push-started him. Back on the test bench, Ricardo had applied a brake to the engines to achieve a similar effect. Every time that Green ran on Wednesday morning, the rear engine reached its 400°, the boost came in, and JCB Dieselmax pulled like a train dumping a bunch of hobos.

But not on the salt on the first run that Thursday.

They had gone back to the course on Wednesday afternoon full of hope, only to be stymied by the crosswinds. But they had remained confident. Then they'd had to wait in line on Thursday with everyone else, the tension ramping up. Then there were two serious accidents. It was not until 13.42 that Dieselmax and the Fastrac went into their routine, and moments later the streamliner

was reported to have achieved only 70mph in the first mile and to be cruising to a halt, even though Green had again done everything he could think of. Same problem.

The latest failure was an unexpected slap in the face, lent added sting as the official timer joked yet again that the Fastrac seemed likely to overtake Dieselmax. The overriding feeling in the trailer was numbness. Beasley in particular sat shaking his head in disbelief, gutted like all of his colleagues by the vicious persistence of a problem that should no longer have existed.

The men who had brought life to the dramatic machine were as close to despair as their calm engineering temperaments were ever likely to allow them to get.

As they watched footage of the run, Green described how he made several attempts to get both temperatures equalised. The front engine's exhaust temperature was 650°C, the rear engine's only 450°C, proof that the front engine was still overpowering the rear.

With so many computer-monitored systems and the need to pre-heat the engines, JCB Dieselmax was always accompanied by its generator trailer.

Bond chases Green during further tests at Wendover Airfield.

↓ The presence of the airfield so close to the hangar was a boon as Green made many test runs chasing the boost gremlin.

'I was still really angry that such a small thing had caused us so much grief. It was sort of, "Why us? Why do we get all the problems!?"'

**Matt Beasley**

'We need to check the balance pipe,' Beasley suggested, white-faced.

'The engines are clearly very sensitive to atmospheric pressure,' Leverton said.

They were still mulling things over, getting more and more frustrated, when deliverance from the haunting spectre of failure arrived in the form of Richard Cornwell, one of Ricardo's data technicians.

'It's a software problem!' he declared. 'The rear engine thought it was in neutral at 2,100rpm, so it was doing exactly what it was designed to do, only fuelling the engine to 2,100rpm if the gearbox was in neutral...'

'How much bad luck can we have?' Beasley snarled, unappeased. Nobody answered. There was no answer. Then Leverton summarised the feelings of relief and frustration with one word: 'Bollocks.'

The software problem was a simple fault in the complex electronics. The rear engine's management system thought the driveline was in neutral and had accordingly restricted the engine's performance. The system was refusing to acknowledge the rear gearbox controller's assurance that the rear driveline was actually in gear, so it was not allowing the rear engine's boost to become established.

For Beasley, even that development was not enough to assuage his anger. He was momentarily beyond seeking or feeling relief. As Green admitted, 'We were all sitting there in that meeting, not saying it but willing old "Max Diesel" to get his side of things sorted out.'

Beasley had been under intense pressure since January when the engine development programme really began to gather pace, and felt it very personally that the more serious problems Dieselmax had encountered on the salt appeared to fall within his purlieu.

'It was great that Richard had given us the answer,' he admitted, 'but I was still really angry that such a small thing had caused us so much grief. It was sort of, "Why us? Why do we get all the problems?"'

'I went for a ten-minute walk towards the Silver Island

The persistent failure to establish boost on both engines reached critical mass on August 17th, ramping up the tension every time the car ran.

Mountains to cool off, but eventually gave up when I didn't seem to be making any progress!'

His reaction was typical of the people who worked on the project. People such as Mark Davies who was the front engine mechanic, or Martin Broadhurst, his oppo on the rear unit, and Ricardo technicians Mark Guy and Michael Chapman. Or data engineer Teena Gade, who was so determined to get a job that she pestered Piper at Visioneering until the JCB opportunity finally came up. Or Rob Millar, whose RDVS company had designed and installed the electrical system and the unique lithium

iron lightweight batteries. All of them believed so passionately in the project, and none of them wanted to let their team-mates down. Keeping up to the mark was like some sort of badge of honour. There is no price for that sort of commitment.

Suddenly the mood had lifted. The problem had been identified. By 16.52, the hottest part of the day, JCB Dieselmax was rolling again. This time Green left the Fastrac far behind as he bulleted on to the horizon against a 10mph headwind. And the timer's calm intonation over the CB radio told the story: entry speed into the first mile 240.792mph, average for the first mile 254.733; second mile average 285.277, third mile average 308.252. Exit speed 313.584.

Joyce Jensen, wife of Bonneville starter Jim Jensen, summarised it perfectly in that laconic way of Americans. As the speeds came over she whooped: 'The computer finally got smart!'

Ultimately it mattered not that Green had exceeded his run profile by 20mph and lost his first braking parachute (he expected that, having discovered that a supplier had not allowed for any safety margin in the strop). The car came to rest safely via its exhaust brake and the second 'chute, which he deployed at lower speed. There was a mood of euphoria in the camp, and the run qualified them for a return attempt the following day, under the rules that apply at Speed Week.

'The car was pulling like a train and it behaved perfectly, with virtually zero wheelspin,' Green reported. 'I could feel it moving around a little at maximum speed but it remained very controllable and performed comfortably within its capacity of going well over 300mph, and we were not flat out today. I'm happy with the run.'

Down the course, with Piper, Leverton again had only one word to say: 'Yeeeeeehah!'

'John and I positioned ourselves at the end of the course to receive the car so that John could evaluate the tyres immediately it had stopped, so that was where we were around 11.30. We witnessed a streamliner spinning at 250mph plus in the fifth mile so that it was travelling backwards along the track for a moment before going end over end and breaking up over a distance of a quarter of a mile. A sobering reminder of what can happen

The format of Speed Week necessitated long waits in line before JCB Dieselmax was clear to run.

→ **Fast, stable and reliable, JCB Dieselmax heads down the salt on the opening run that counted towards its first record.**

↓ **The relief was palpable: Jon Oakey and another team member celebrate hitting 300mph.**

when it goes wrong at those sort of speeds. Thankfully the driver was okay.

'We were at the 6.5 mile point for Andy's afternoon run. The senior steward said, "Heads up everyone, the JCB 'liner is coming down next." They only say that for the quickest cars and they took us just as seriously that time as for all our other runs.

'I was waiting to note down the speeds on my pad. By the end my hand was shaking as we could see the car travelling at over 300mph in front of us.'

In their haste to get back to the pits the duo leapt into a red Dodge Durango and struggled to get it fired up until they realised they had got into the wrong car. JCB had hired four of them... They didn't feel so bad later when they learned that one morning with ThrustSSC at Black Rock Noble had inadvertently run over his own laptop...

Back in the pits there were handshakes and hugs all round. The stress and tension had been annihilated by the burst of speed. Leverton admitted that he was left speechless, and he wasn't the only one. Back at the startline, the sizeable crowd was cheering along with the Brits. They'd been rooting for the streamliner all week, and now it had delivered and justified their faith. It was the 48th run Dieselmax had ever made.

Under the rules the car had to go into impound overnight,

When not running under its own power, Dieselmax was manoeuvred around by a JCB Groundhog. Eoin Corrigan later used one to set a record of 18.079mph.

One word can mean so much. The Impound area sign signified that Dieselmax had qualified for a crack at Roy Lewis's national diesel-power record.

where it could be worked on only to a limited extent, prior to making a back-up run the next day. The pressure was squarely on Green as JCB Dieselmax headed back down the salt at 08.57 the following morning. He admitted that he had fudged one gearshift the previous day, that having selected fifth he needed to go back to fourth momentarily to maintain momentum. But this day's earlier start gave him better conditions with firmer salt and less effect from the altitude, and he was on top of his game. He entered the first mile at 249.286mph and averaged 268.694 through it; the second was devoured at 304.134; the third at a remarkable 325.791 with a 334mph exit speed.

Poor Roy Lewis's reign was over; Green and JCB Dieselmax averaged 317.021mph for a new SCTA-BNI diesel land speed record.

And there was more. Green kept his foot down and exited mile six at a peak speed of 354...

'Actually,' he grinned, 'I was busy doing an instrument check and when I looked up and saw a mile marker flash by I thought, "Was that the measured mile or not?" So I just kept my foot down in case it wasn't, just to be sure.

'I was comfortable doing that because the car was very well made and handled superbly. I could trust it completely. Keeping it straight and putting down the power proved much easier than we had thought, with only minor steering corrections needed and little adjustment to the throttle. But the Palmer training paid off – a small correction not made can become a very big correction a few seconds later, so a good feel for the car's behaviour was very useful. Every car moves around on the salt, particularly under hard acceleration or crosswinds – even Dieselmax. Look how many cars spin out at 200+ mph. I could feel the tyres scrabbling for grip on occasion and sometimes slipping on the softer parts of the track, while the car moved around on the slightly uneven surface and drifted sideways with the crosswinds. And this was against the background of the two loudest diesel engines in the world! At idle and low speed, the vibration and noise was tremendous, becoming a howling whine when they came on to boost – but boy was that a great feeling, when the car would take off like a scalded cat.

'You know, there were two things, coming here. The big

Man and machine: Dr Tim Leverton, with the car he fought so hard to create.

concern was not to go messing about just optimising development work in Speed Week thinking we'd always get a record next week, and then finding some critical problem with the car and not being able to run again. Suddenly we wouldn't have had a record, and that would have been so disappointing.

'And secondly, we were aware that we really didn't merely want to use Speed Week to develop the car and not take part in the principles here which are driving fast and setting records. We've taken part properly, as competitors, and have the option of further development next week. It couldn't be better.'

Green was feted by a team high on adrenaline – and relief. Perhaps the happiest man was also the least demonstrative. Ron Ayers, who made supersonic speed on land a possibility and who boldly decided to forego wind tunnel tests and to stride again into uncharted territory by relying purely on computational fluid dynamics in the design of the car, allowed himself a quiet smile and encouraged people to have a look beneath the streamliner. The underside was totally devoid of salt build-up, testimony to the effectiveness of his clever aerodynamic design that minimised spray drag.

In fact, JCB Dieselmax performed so well that perspectives changed. One thing was now crystal clear. When they ran for the official FIA international diesel record the following week the primary limiting factor wasn't going to be horsepower, aerodynamics or rolling resistance, as originally thought, but tyre technology. Green had set the record still running the 600bhp engines that had done all of the previous testing. The 750bhp race versions were still held in reserve. The improved climatic and course conditions had made a huge difference, and it was clear that with another 25 per cent power, even allowing for the fact that drag rises with the square of the speed, the car had significantly greater potential than its 350mph tyre limitation.

Sir Anthony Bamford said it all when Leverton called him with the news that his engines now powered the world's fastest diesel car.

'Absolutely bloody marvellous!'

As feats of British engineering go, this was right up there with the very best. But it was only the beginning.

↓ **Preparing for the all-important return run.**

↑ **Annie Berrisford and Chris Dee lost no time amending the team poster once Green's 317mph record was confirmed.**

↓ **JCB Dieselmax ran beautifully on the return run. Green averaged 325.971mph to clinch his new SCTA/BNI national record of 317.021mph.**

THE WORLD'S FASTEST DIESEL

# CHAPTER 12
# PASSING ROUND THE HAT

Later on that morning of 17 August, a small ceremony took place by the impound pen on the salt as Larry Volk and SCTA-BNI Advisory Board Member Dan Warner presented Andy Green with his blue 300 MPH Chapter hat and a t-shirt, before Carolyn Sager handed over his unlimited Bonneville racing licence. Green swapped his yellow JCB shirt for the t-shirt, and made a gracious acceptance speech which conveyed just what the achievement meant to a man who only now felt that he had fully earned his land speed racing spurs.

'As an honorary member of the 200 MPH Club (300 MPH Chapter), I was acutely aware that, since the late '20s, I was the only holder of the world land speed record never to have driven at Bonneville. That has now changed – and how! I am now a full member of the 300 MPH Chapter and very proud of the fact. To give you some idea of how this feels, consider this: well over 1,000 human beings have climbed Everest, about 450 have been into space and about the same number are members of the 200 MPH Club, which makes the 300 MPH Chapter (around 68 members) far more exclusive than either climbing Everest or going into space. And populated by much more interesting people....'

That evening, as the team celebrated its triumph, Tim Leverton took the 300 MPH Chapter cap and insisted that every team member should touch it. 'It's important that we all appreciate what this represents,' he said quietly, 'and that you are each members of a great team that helped Andy to take his place with this elite.'

Later, he added: 'We'd had all of the elation of Friday and that night we went for a quiet dinner with Andy and Sophy and Richard. And Andy had his hat on. I realised that he must be one of the very few people to have been made an honorary member of the 300 Chapter, and then to have come back and won the hat as a full member. So I sat at the dinner table for a while with it on! It was pretty cool, actually...

'Then we went back to the Peppermill and then Black and White, preparing for an early night. But probably two-thirds of the team were in the sunken bar at the Peppermill. That was one of the things about this team: they worked hard together all day, and then chose to spend their free time together.

'We were sitting there, discussing what it all meant to them. Very personal comments. And I just thought about what I'd felt wearing that hat. So I said to Andy, "If you don't object, they should all try it on." They all wanted to, but none of them would have asked. Once they started putting it on I could see that it was doing for them the same thing it had done to me. They had their photographs taken wearing it.'

The plan now was to take out the 600bhp 'runway' engines, which had been impressively reliable, and replace them with the pukka 750bhp 'race' versions over the weekend. By Sunday morning, the 20th, both had been installed. It normally took 10 hours to do an engine change, but Beasley explained: 'We are taking perhaps a little longer because we are making some improvements to the cooling, fuel and oil systems that we couldn't do while the old engines were in place.'

A party of journalists had been flown out from the UK and arrived on Wednesday, 21 August, just in time to see Dieselmax leaking oil and fuel in its Wendover hangar. It is sod's law that such things always happen in the full glare of publicity. Both problems were simple, but awkward to fix.

'We had a low-pressure fuel supply issue last week,' Beasley explained. 'We fixed that, but the way we fixed it was by raising the fuel pressure. We hadn't turned that back down and when we just switched on the front engine today it was still high enough to pop an oil seal, flooding the engine with fuel and oil. There's also a small oil leak, too, an associated problem. An o-ring seal was slightly imperfect. It would be dead easy to fix it all with the engine out; as it is the cover plate access is not exactly user-friendly.'

By the following day everything was set for the first attempt on Virgil Snyder's 235.756mph FIA international diesel record. The omens were good. It was John Piper's birthday, and he had moved the previous night into a new room at the Rainbow Hotel. The 444 Bonneville registration number was already allocated to Nish Motorsports, but it was still a neat touch that JCB Dieselmax was registered as 440 AA/DS, meaning that it ran in the unlimited

↑ **Sir Anthony Bamford arrived on the salt on August 22, just in time to see his dream come true of an international land speed record for his JCB444 diesel engine.**

← **Green's Bonneville 200mph Club 300mph Chapter hat, a very special symbol of excellence.**

JCB engineer Steve Lewis continues the final preparations on JCB Dieselmax, over the weekend of August 19/20.

That was when a group of British journalists was flown out. Matt Beasley gives them the rundown on the technology.

Mark Guy replenishes the vital fluids after the 'race' engines had been installed.

'Back when we did the deal with JCB, and we had worked out
various dates, I remember John [Piper] turning to me and saying,
"I'd really like to do the record on my birthday..."'

**Brian Horner**

**Green checks the parachutes (above) and prepares for action (below).**

diesel streamliner class. Piper's new room was number 440... 'Back when we did the deal with JCB,' Brian Horner recalled, 'and we had worked out various dates, I remember John turning to me and saying, "I'd really like to do the record on my birthday..."'

The day's run plan called for a warm-up run and then two passes for the record. But there was another false start when a minor electrical glitch stopped the car. Two wires had been crimped together when the cockpit canopy was closed, and that triggered a circuit breaker. The problem was quickly fixed.

At 09.37 the first pukka run began, and it was a very good one, clearly not a warm-up after all. Green entered the mile at 319mph and exited around 328, for an average of 324.265mph. The record was a genuine possibility straight away.

The international course had now been graded three times by Wes Hutchens, a final pass over that morning serving just to 'polish' the surface. During the turnaround, Green told BNI president Mike Cook: 'What a great course! You guys have done a wonderful job!'

The salt was even better than it had been the previous Friday, because of the earlier start. At the north-east end it was a little wetter than at the south-western starting point, and stuck to the soles of your shoes more, but it was very firm.

Green talked happily about the run as the crew serviced the car. 'The interesting thing is that in Mile 4 we were really pulling but were thermally limited after that. We haven't quite limited the engines where we want them.

'The rolling resistance is still low – I expected to coast down to the depot at Mile 11 but was still doing 200mph with a mile and a half left to run. It's nice when stopping is more of a problem than getting going! I didn't get any wheelspin this time. I was looking for it in first gear, but there wasn't any. It might be a problem this end, though...'

He still hadn't used sixth gear, and hadn't bothered with the parachute.

This was the first time the crew had done a turnaround. There had been no time to practice because they'd been rebuilding the car. Yet after 40 minutes of the allotted hour everything was ready. The wheels and tyres had been changed, what little salt had

← **The JCB team could not have asked for
better salt or weather conditions on the
morning of August 22nd, 2006.**

been thrown into the wheel spats had been removed, the engines
had been pre-heated and the ice coolant and fuel had been
replenished. It was an impressive performance.

At 10.25 Dieselmax was fired up, and after a short delay due
to radio communications problems between Startline and
Control had been solved, Bond moved Fastrac in for the push-
start. There were still 12 minutes left of the hour as Green
headed south-west.

As before, he found the engines were thermally limited, but
it was the best run yet – 333.364mph. The overall average was
328.767mph, and Snyder's 33-year-old record had been consigned
to history. Green and JCB Dieselmax had added almost
100mph to it.

Watching in the mile, Jack Franck, who had been with
ThrustSSC, turned enthusiastically to Richard Noble. 'I tell you,
that thing sounded like a Mustang P51 with 100 inches of boost!'
To which Noble replied: 'Jack, it's got 180 inches!'

As Green climbed from the cockpit he was surrounded by
whooping team members, and the congratulations fluttered
through the air like confetti at a wedding. The team was inevitably
posed for victory shots, and an impromptu Happy Birthday
chorus broke out in honour of Piper.

'We have the fastest diesel car in the world. We have done
exactly what we came to do,' Green told reporters with a smile
as wide as the desert, his voice still in that fast-paced but clipped
mode of the test pilot. 'This is British engineering at its absolute
best. To set two records in a total of four runs, with a rebuild in
the middle, is an astonishing team and engineering achievement.'

Sir Anthony Bamford and his family had flown in that morning,
and the Chairman's smile was perhaps even broader as he shook
Green's hand. He then made a point of doing the same with
every crew member.

'First I would like to thank you for having the courage to do
this,' Green told him, 'because it was a big thing to do. And
secondly I'd like to thank you for letting me do it. Thirdly, thank
you for letting this team show just what they can achieve. They've
done brilliant work, all of them.'

Bamford was of no mind to disagree. It was a year to the day

'The rolling resistance is still low – I expected to coast down to the depot at Mile 11 but was still doing 200mph with a mile and a half left to run. It's nice when stopping is more of a problem than getting going! I didn't get any wheelspin this time. I was looking for it in first gear, but there wasn't any. It might be a problem this end, though...'

**Andy Green**

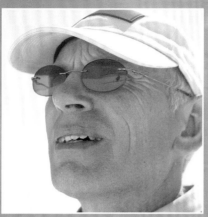

↑ More of the tight-knit team behind the success of JCB Dieselmax: Dave Brown, HI Project Manager; Steve Lewis, Transmission Engineer; Mark Guy, Senior Engine Test Technician; Daniel Ward, Project Communications and JCB World Communications Manager; Duffy Sheardown, Programme Manager; Alastair Macqueen, Race Engineer; Teena Gade, Data Acquisition/ Electrical System Engineer; and David Hoyle, Transmissions Manager.

Congratulations were the order of the morning: Andy Green with John Patterson, JCB's Managing Director and CEO.

Within minutes of the August 22nd runs, the tail of JCB Dieselmax bore another telltale decal.

Safe seat: Rob Millar and Colin Bond hold Green aloft as he celebrates with team-mates Jon Oakey, Sir Anthony Bamford, girlfriend Sophy Gardner, Mike Chapman, Rod Benoist and Brian Horner.

since Tim Leverton had led his little explorative expedition to Speed Week, and now they had achieved their goal comfortably.

'It's thrilling,' Bamford said, his body language signalling his pleasure. 'Better than I could have expected, and it was only a dummy run to begin with. It's a blow for British engineering, it shows we can do it, and that we can do a great job. We have the fastest diesel car and engine in the world. This was brilliant teamwork in adversity, we have seen how many heartaches they got through so well.'

As the celebrations continued, Australia's answer to Noble, Rosco McGlashan, paid a visit to congratulate the team. And within an hour of the success a 328.767mph decal had joined the 317.021mph on the tail of the streamliner. At the same time, the car's trailer also bore new signs proclaiming it the world's fastest diesel. It wasn't just the car that moved fast.

When things had quietened down a little, Green expanded on the return run. 'The coolant was still overheating, and that in turn affected the exhaust temperature which therefore affected the boost. It happened while I was in fourth, which is the most important gear. I calculate that we used only 1,000 of our 1,500bhp. We were running in Cal 2 mode as the system trimmed the engines back to 500 when they started to nudge the thermal limit. We need to open up the cooling a little, as the coolant is still cold at the end of each run.'

'It would have been faster if I had remembered actually to cruise through the measured mile rather than start slowing down. I was still in development mode and thought, "Fine, we cracked the speed, yeah, everything's fine. Exhaust brake on. Ooops, we're still in the mile."'

Actually he used a slightly stronger expression, before reminding himself on the cockpit voice transmission, 'That was embarrassing.'

But they still had the fastest diesel car in the world, measured by the FIA, the world authority. 'This is a huge statement of just how good the JCB engines really are,' Green added, 'and more importantly British engineering and diesel power have both achieved something quite amazing today. It's been a real privilege to be a part of that.'

He reflected on the paradoxical nature of the car. 'We realised

'We have the fastest diesel car in the world. We have done exactly what we came to do... This is British engineering at its absolute best. To set two records in a total of four runs, with a rebuild in the middle, is an astonishing team and engineering achievement.'

**Andy Green**

In the immediate aftermath of the latest success, Sir Anthony made a point of personally thanking each member of his team.

He then made a heartfelt speech on the salt explaining the motivations behind Britain's latest land speed record venture.

early on that it needed to be hot to work. But ideally you want half the car to be hot while the other half is cool! Now we need the ability to pump the heat faster. We pre-heat the car and then spend the rest of our time trying to cool it down. We need to move an awful lot of heat from one place to another in a hurry.

'The car was even better on the way back. We had no traction problems at all even at the damper end. The car is so well set up with its four-wheel drive that it actually pulls very, very cleanly. Apart from a couple of tiny steering corrections, it was dead straight all the way. And we still didn't get out of fifth gear! We are now looking at a thermal limit and what we can do about that I don't know. That's part of the development engineering. But the car has a lot more capacity. It's incredibly quick. Ron Ayers and John Piper have created an amazing record-breaking platform.'

There was another little insight, into the mind of the speed record breaker and Green the professional pilot. The onboard GPS resolutely got to 223mph and then ceased to register. It had been supplied with automotive software rather than aircraft, and of course what car could be expected to exceed 223?

Green explained this to the assembled media, and said he calculated his speed from the revs and the gear he was in, at 300mph plus. He seemed genuinely surprised when one journalist struggled to imagine anyone doing that, even one with a first in mathematics from Oxford, and launched into a complex explanation of flying fighter aircraft against electronic jammers.

'The jammer may deny a lot of information to the radar, so there are several techniques for deriving information. If the range is jammed but we can see where the jamming is coming from, then a rapid climb/descent to zero the radar elevation will establish the jammer's height. Then a rapid descent by, say, 5,000ft (unless he's at low level, when a rapid climb works better!) will give you a known difference. A simple mental calculation then gives range: when the target is 2 deg up he is at 25nm, at 4 deg up he is at about 12nm, at 5 deg up he is at 10nm, at 6 deg up he is at about 8nm, etc. Careful use of a stopwatch can turn these ranges into approximate closure speeds, which are useful as they affect air-to-air weapon ranges. Subtracting our speed from the closure will then give target speed, which is essential should we need to turn in

**Ron Ayers holds one of Visioneering's scale models of Dieselmax. The great aerodynamicist's innovative theories on spray drag were proved to be spot-on.**

There are few more spectacular places for celebratory dinners after land speed record success than the flats themselves.

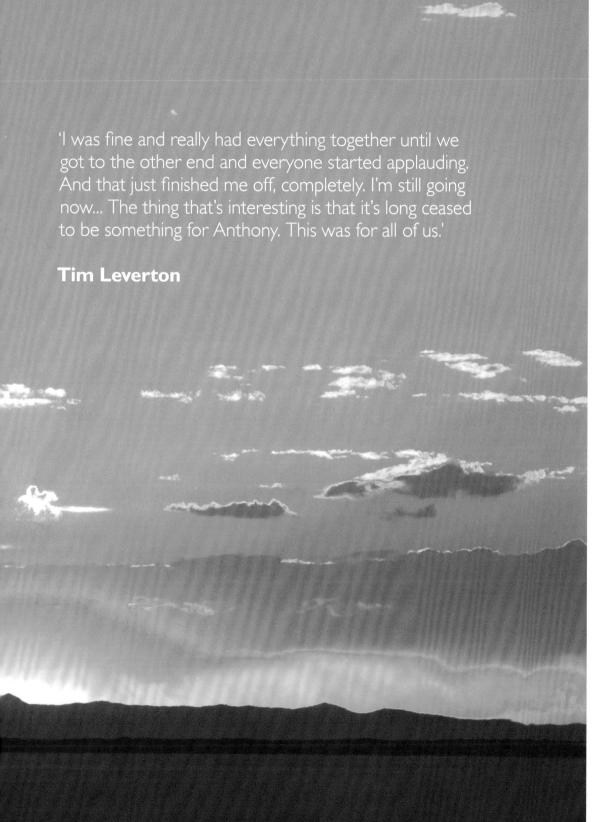

'I was fine and really had everything together until we got to the other end and everyone started applauding. And that just finished me off, completely. I'm still going now... The thing that's interesting is that it's long ceased to be something for Anthony. This was for all of us.'

**Tim Leverton**

behind the target/jammer to identify him. Of course, while all this is going on, a similar process is being carried out in the horizontal plane to determine the jammer's heading, which is also key. These techniques are now largely out of date, but were the sort of thing that I grew up practicing as a young fighter pilot on Phantoms. So working out the speed from the rpm should not have been too difficult...'

Leverton opened up later that day, and admitted at one point that he was tearing up behind his sunglasses even as he spoke. He had gone from a pragmatic engineer, with an engineer's classification of all things as black or white, to a man who had caught salt fever in the best possible way, and who had found emotion creeping in more and more to his everyday life.

'This was the pukka one. I felt just as nervous, and the feeling I had at the end was just the same as it was after the SCTA run.

'I got in the right car this time, but I had trouble starting it as it was still in Drive... I was okay until Anthony cracked up. He had to put his shades back on, put it that way. Actually, I was fine and really had everything together until we got to the other end and everyone started applauding. And that just finished me off, completely. I'm still going now...

'The thing that's interesting is that it's long ceased to be something for Anthony. This was for all of us.'

As so frequently happens with such projects, those who enlist find themselves appropriating the prime mover's dream as their own, such is the intensity of the passion they develop for it. That was precisely what happened with the JCB Dieselmax team. One man's dream became their religion.

Like Guy Vandervell, the '50s industrialist who created the Vanwall cars that put Britain on the Formula One map, Sir Anthony Bamford is not known as a great externaliser. But after his moment with his shades there was another sign when he was presented with one of Brian Horner's superb models of the streamliner, one of only 10 in the world. Bamford wouldn't let anyone put it back in its packing case but insisted on taking it with him on his jet.

Such passion ran through the project from the highest to the lowest, which was one reason why this was such a cohesive record attempt. Everybody got along, and everybody cared.

# CHAPTER 13

# PROJECT HI COMES OF AGE

The decision to go for 350mph was not taken lightly. Not with a man's life at stake if somebody else let their enthusiasm overrule their judgement.

'Alastair's ability to see the bigger picture of everything that is going on is impressive,' Tim Leverton said of Alastair Macqueen. 'He came to me to talk through the run profile on Friday, which was to go through 330, 340, 350 and 360mph, and we all walked away from the meeting, and I thought, "I'm not really happy with that, because the tyres are good for 350 on the rig and we think they are good for 350 on the salt, but we are into completely new territory." And by Saturday morning, Alastair, John and I, over a cup of coffee, realised that all three of us had had the same feeling, which was that we should focus on 350. One of the things with good teams is when you can have short conversations. When you can just say what you think and the other guys know what you mean. That's happened so many times when we've decided something, then we've come back and a couple of us have asked questions of each other and we've quickly modified what we want to do, to a new level on which we are unified. That's unusual.

'On the tyres it was a matter of saying that's what we are prepared to do and that's where we are prepared to stop.'

For Wednesday's runs, lower rated thermostats were installed in Dieselmax's cooling system, and a bleed hole incorporated to make them respond faster. The restrictor in the water circulation was also biased to allow the front engine to run a little cooler.

Everyone was on the desert by six o'clock that morning, 23rd August. It was calm and quiet and dark, cold enough still for jumpers.

By 07.37 JCB Dieselmax was rolling. The atmosphere was tense. The 350mph goal remained unspoken by all, but everyone knew it was there. Then the radio crackled: 365.745mph through the mile! And that was with a nine mile an hour crosswind running from the Silver Island Mountains.

Green was delighted as he climbed out at the south-western depot. 'That was better! Both engines heated up okay. The front was 15°C cooler, though, than yesterday. And I was still in fifth,

albeit close to the rev limit. Traction was super, just a little bit of feedback in the second to third mile, where the international course crosses the national course. The car is so stable, I barely felt the crosswind. Just made tiny steering corrections.

'At the end of the measured mile, I put the exhaust brakes on and, once the car had slowed to 300mph, put out the chute. It was a clean and successful deployment – our development programme on the chutes had worked perfectly.

'To be honest I'm not surprised at the speed; I wanted 335 and when I got there I trimmed it back, but the throttle lag was a factor and we actually picked up another few miles an hour before it had its effect.'

Piper checked the tyres, which had already been changed, looking for blisters, any outward sign of heat build up. There was none. They looked almost new, even the sprue pips from the mould hadn't been worn off. 'They're still cold,' he reported, a gleam in his eye. 'It looks good. That's what happens to LSR tyres if you put suspension on the car – they don't have to work so hard.'

The tension began building again as the time for Green's return run approached. This was only the second turnaround the crew had done, yet this time it was over in 40 minutes.

At 08.16 the sun was higher in the sky now, with just a gentle wind. Five minutes later, Green and Dieselmax were rolling.

As soon as the car left the line everyone bolted for their cars to chase him back to the south-west end. But then came the problem as they hit 100mph and found themselves beginning to haul in the streamliner when it should have been bulleting on to the horizon. Once again the spectre of failure hovered over the yellow and black car as it stammered down the course, eating up precious run-up area at pitiful speed. The chase cars backed off to 80, anxious not to get ahead, and alongside Macqueen in their Durango Matt Beasley screamed obscenities at the car in which he had invested so much of himself. He wasn't the only one. Then, suddenly, Dieselmax picked up her skirts and began to fly. Soon it had disappeared. But how much damage had been done to the average for the two runs?

**Tension was high on the flats in the early dawn of Wednesday, August 23rd, as everyone was aware that 350mph was getting close to the limit of Dieselmax's tyre rating.**

Then the speed came over the radio: 335.695 mph through the mile. Everybody started doing the frantic maths, but it was more complicated than adding the speeds and dividing by two. The FIA calculates the elapsed times for the measured distance, then divides them and calculates the speed from the result. Had they done it?

And then, even before crew members spilled from their cars to rush over to Dieselmax and Green, who was standing as calmly as ever alongside it, the radio crackled another figure: average speed 350.092mph. They had done it, by nine-hundredths of a mile an hour! This time it was engineer Teena Gade who got the birthday present. She thought it was better than the one Piper got.

'That was fantastic!' Green beamed, the news already relayed to him. 'I'm so pleased that we got the car to what was only ever the maximum aspirational run speed, and that with a problematic start and so much more to come. It was still pulling like a train once I got it going, and I still haven't used sixth gear. It's got so much to give, this car. It's fantastic! Now all we need is new tyres, to make it go a lot faster.'

'Besides the mile record, JCB Dieselmax also took the kilometre. The speed was slightly faster, at 350.452mph, but the FIA convention has always been, where both distance records have been secured, to take the longer one as the record speed.

Final preparations prior to fitting the bodywork (left) and yet more ice (above).

↓**Leverton briefs the troops before the push to the final summit of the Dieselmax project's aspirations.**

Dieselmax took only 9.842s to speed through the mile on its first run, 10.724s for its second. That fractional difference was sufficient to rob the car of 30mph.

So what had gone wrong? It was the old bugbear.

'The rear engine exhaust temperature was about 600°C but the front was down to 250°C,' Green explained, 'so it just needed another 10 seconds on the brake. Then it was away. It was the same problem we had last week. The changes to the cooling system worked so well that the front engine arrived at the north-eastern end 20°C colder than it had previously been. It just sat there then and we deliberately didn't preheat it much so we had a bit more thermal inertia in the system, so the front engine was as cold as it had ever been when we set off.

'The combination of that and the lower water jacket temperature was just enough to make it struggle on boost. I had the boost indication as 1.2 on both, pushed it up to 2.5, and the rear started to lead. That was unusual. The front balanced out, they got to about 1.3, and I would guess the balance pipe was now sharing the boost between the two engines. Then the rear engine picked up and took all the load and the front cooled down. We'd seen this before. I figured it was a dead run at that stage. I didn't have time to do anything else, so it was a case of dragging the brakes, trying to cook it up, getting the front engine back up above 400, and then sure enough, once it finally started picking up it did so strongly. I managed to get it back on boost, but it cost me almost a mile. After that it was a case of driving it right to the rev limiter in everything but sixth gear, which we still haven't used! I did it once when the car was on stands, just to check it's there!'

He admitted that he'd thought it was a dead run, and that the 365 opening pass would be wasted. Macqueen had thought the same, and both men had mentally shifted focus to the following day.

'I began to feel hugely disappointed for all of the guys,' Green said. 'Would we have to come back and do two runs tomorrow? The expectation after we'd just done a 365 run was that we'd got to get a 350 out of this. And of course it was a development car, there was always the chance of some little niggle, we'd

↓ The start of Dieselmax's penultimate run at Bonneville, heading for 365mph through the measured mile.

THE WORLD'S FASTEST DIESEL

'Traction was super; just a little bit of feedback in the second to third mile. The car is so stable, I barely felt the crosswind. Just made tiny steering corrections.'

**Andy Green**

change something that would have an unintended consequence. That's classic record-breaking, that highs and lows bit. But fortunately this time it was only about a minute long rather than the usual 24 hours long.'

There were more revelations. He had carried a guardian angel broach in his pocket. 'It's a good luck symbol from the El Mirage Ladies Auxiliary,' explained Mike Cook, whose wife Penny came up with the idea. 'A little spirit of the good side of life.' He'd also been asked to carry a squirrel called Speedy, a salt mascot owned by timers Alan and James Rice which had been all over the world and had also hitched a ride in the Honda F1 car a few weeks earlier when Alan van der Merwe achieved 248mph on the salt. 'Don't you dare mention Donald Campbell!' Green laughed, in reference to the famed speedking's superstitions.

Beasley and Leverton admitted to mixed emotions.

'It wasn't better than the other two, to be honest,' said 'Max Diesel'. 'The first run went exactly to plan, I'm very happy with that. The cooling system worked better than ever, but that caught us out on the return run. We put just a little bit of preheat on, up to 70°C, as the engines were so much cooler, and it took Andy nearly two miles to get on boost. If we'd preheated them up to a little more, up to 80 again, we'd have been on boost in a mile, mile and a half, and we would have had a repeat run. So it's a bit of a shame. But it was just the right side of 350mph.'

Leverton heard over the radio that Green wanted to abort and go back to the start. 'I thought, "Shit," because that would mean we'd lose the hour, for sure. Your heart goes... Then I could suddenly see the car start moving and I knew immediately what had happened. And then to go from Mile 8 into the mile at, what, 335 or something, and out at 345, and then just to get 0.092 the right side of 350 – fantastic! How cool is that?

'It's a different feeling from yesterday. We've had six runs and three records now, and since we got the car running in the way we wanted it to this is the first time that it hasn't performed properly.

'The tyres look great, we've got a bit of pressure to continue. But we'll just go and have a calm think. I'm not prepared to agree to anything without going through it all.'

Subsequently, he explained why he called a halt after Project H1 had come of age.

'The 350.092mph FIA record accomplished all the objectives of this phase of our project. That is why when we reached 350mph I decided to stop. We now knew that JCB Dieselmax's speed capability was tyre limited.

'It was a strange feeling taking the decision to finish. None of us really wanted it all to come to an end even though we knew it would. As John Piper said to me, in a race a chap stands there and waves a chequered flag and it's all over. In land speed racing the decision is your own how far you go.'

'Everything up to now has validated the car up to the planned 350,' Alastair Macqueen said. 'Stopping is a very sensible decision. The car performed beautifully and so did the engines, and they left enough evidence that it will go faster.

'From the commercial, engineering, safety and emotional sides – once we are all down from the adrenaline rush and salt fever – we'll all see it as the right decision. And the longer time goes by the more I'm confident it was. And it was unanimous. We all had the same reservations about stopping – here we were with what was perhaps a once in a lifetime opportunity. What might conditions be like in 2007? We believe the car can do 400, and the real reason for stopping now would be to come back next year, and we'd be more likely to do that if a bigger jump was still available.

'I think we all ultimately felt that we'd rather take a risk on Tim being able to persuade Sir Anthony to find a tyre partner and let us come back, than we would to run tomorrow and risk Andy.'

There was, however, another record for JCB to secure. The timing gear was still set up, and that afternoon the two JCB Groundhogs were brought out. JCB engineer Steve Lewis and Eoin Corrigan took their machines twice through the miles. Corrigan was faster at 18.079mph for the mile even though he suffered an early parachute deployment (a JCB umbrella held out of the rear window) which he was sure cost him 0.1mph.

There was also some film work to be done on the Thursday, mainly close-up tracking shots of JCB Dieselmax which would be pushed to 40mph and then left to coast down without the engines running. Green delegated the driving to Leverton and Piper. 'I was

↓ His initial boost problems behind him, Green gets his
foot down as he desperately tries to keep his average speed
up on JCB Dieselmax's final record run at Bonneville.

'The rear engine exhaust temperature was about 600°C but
the front was down to 250°C, so it just needed another 10
seconds on the brake. Then it was away. It was the same
problem we had last week.'

**Andy Green**

thrilled not only to have the chance to sit in the driver's seat but also to be able to say that I was Andy Green's body double!' the former said. 'I don't know if there is a career in this for me – apparently he wants to do his own stunts...

'In the car you can only see forward at a limited angle and you have to focus on the horizon to know where to steer. It rolls along very easily at 40mph for ages, only gradually dropping speed over half a mile or so. It seems to have virtually no rolling resistance. After two pushes I realised why Andy did not want to be stuck in there. My shirt was soaked and I could hardly breathe. But it was a lot of fun and everyone got their chance over three hours of filming, which shared the heat burden around the team.'

It was the perfect way to wind down after the elation of the previous runs, but the question remained in the back of most minds. Would they go back to Bonneville?

Ricardo's Ian Penny had calculated that JCB Dieselmax used only 1,300 of its 1,500bhp to average 365mph through the mile on the first of its Wednesday runs. But further calculations

suggested the need for a little more power, a bit less weight and a reduction in drag coefficient, as well as new tyres, to push through the 400 barrier. That remained a tantalising thought.

'The team has certainly caught a strong dose of salt fever and we know the car is faster than its tyres,' Leverton said. 'So much will depend on how we could solve that problem. We will review all the engineering results on the project on our return to the UK, and reflect on what is possible before making any decision.' But he added: 'From everything we've seen so far, this looks like a 400mph car. And if it is a 400mph car, then the compulsion to continue to run it is very high. But you need the tyres. And if you are going to make that step to run it, then you don't start taking risks with the existing tyres. You get a proper tyre and then you come back.'

The last runs proved conclusively that JCB Dieselmax still had unfulfilled potential. But regardless of what the future might hold, a very special team had written another fabulous chapter in the story of British endeavour and high achievement in land speed record-breaking.

# POSTSCRIPT

Breaking the diesel land speed record will have important repercussions for JCB. Besides the extraordinary publicity that the bold adventure generated, the company will use the technical lessons to create even better products for the future, a genuine case of motor racing improving the breed.

'There are two possible future directions for the engine,' Tim Leverton suggested. 'One could be marine, and one could be military. We are finding out what the limits are.'

Sir Anthony Bamford said: 'For JCB it is obviously a very valuable thing, great for publicity and because it shows the capabilities of our engines.

'I believe that British engineers are fantastic, that our team of engineers have done a great job. In Britain we don't laud our engineers enough. To me they are a very important part of our team. We employ over 200 engineering graduates and try to recruit every year and to give them actual jobs to do. Some have been involved in this very exciting project.

'The JCB444-LSR engine has opened our eyes to many derivatives of our existing engine and given us more confidence to go on and do other things. In honour of its achievements at Bonneville, we have retitled the engine JCB DIESELMAX.

'One of the technical benefits of this project is that we are able to generate a lot more power out of our existing family of diesel engines, probably more than we realised, so that's a big plus. If, for instance, our products could use four-cylinder engines instead of six-cylinder engines, in certain places it would be better for the customer. I think that is something that is quite realistic, that has come out of the project, and that wouldn't have done otherwise.'

Andy Green was impressed by the company's courage. 'They achieved a lot as a company and I wish there were more like them around. It was also a huge, bold statement on a global stage about the excellence of British engineering. Bloody well done, guys!'

Not to be outdone by the ThrustSSC team, which left the Black Rock Desert cleaner than it had been, JCB cleared up a lot of heavy junk that had been bothering Bonneville regulars for years, once Dieselmax's official business was over.

JCB DIESELMAX JCB

## APPENDIX
# SPECIFICATIONS

**JCB Dieselmax technical specifications**

| | |
|---|---|
| **Engines:** | Two JCB444 common rail injection diesels, bored and stroked to 5,000cc, dry sumped and inclined at 10 degrees from the horizontal, twin compound turbochargers with twin compound intercoolers, ice tank cooling (capacity 200 litres) |
| **Power:** | 750bhp (560Kw) at 3,800rpm |
| **Torque:** | 1,105lb ft (1,500Nm) at 2,000rpm |
| **Fuel tank capacity:** | 15 litres |
| **Transmission:** | Forward transmission and final drive connected to forward engine; rear transmission and final drive connected to rear engine; six-speed barrel-shift transmissions driven through torsional dampers and oil-immersed multi-plate clutches |
| **Steering:** | Rack and pinion, to front wheels |
| **Brakes:** | Split circuit; unique design carbon rotors and twin stators; exhaust brakes for front and rear engines, manually operated; twin parachutes |
| **Suspension:** | Independent all round via twin wishbones, coil springs and hydraulic dampers |
| **Chassis:** | Hybrid square steel tube spaceframe with bonded carbon composite panels |
| **Body:** | Aerodynamically designed – CdA <0.15; carbon composite materials |
| **Wheels and tyres:** | 23x15, Goodyear |

**Dimensions**

| | |
|---|---|
| **Length:** | 9,091mm |
| **Width:** | 1,145mm |
| **Height:** | 979mm to top of canopy, at run speed; 1,337mm to top of fin |
| **Front track:** | 800mm |
| **Rear track:** | 600mm |
| **Wheelbase:** | 5,878mm |
| **Weight:** | 2,700kg including fuel, oil, ice and water coolant, and driver |

# RUN LOG

## JCB Dieselmax run data

### RAF Wittering

| Run | Date | Time | Speed |
|-----|------|------|-------|
| 1 | 22 July | 14.26 | 61mph |
| 2 | 23 July | 18.17 | 100–120mph |
| 3 | 23 July | 19.10 | 100–120mph |
| 4 | 23 July | 20.15 | 112mph |
| 5 | 24 July | 17.02 | 109mph |
| 6 | 24 July | 18.42 | 127mph |
| 7 | 25 July | 19.35 | 169mph |
| 8 | 26 July | 17.45 | 129mph |
| 9 | 28 July | 17.45 | 126mph |
| 10 | 28 July | 18.22 | 153mph |
| 11 | 28 July | 18.56 | 181mph |
| 12 | 29 July | 15.30 | 40mph |
| 13 | 30 July | 12.05 | Warm-up |
| 14 | 30 July | 12.25 | 153mph |
| 15 | 30 July | 12.56 | 185mph |
| 16 | 30 July | 13.30 | 191mph |
| 17 | 30 July | 16.28 | Warm-up |
| 18 | 30 July | 16.53 | 201mph |
| 19 | 30 July | 17.20 | 191mph |
| 20 | 31 July | 12.35 | Warm-up |
| 21 | 31 July | 13.30 | 181mph |
| 22 | 31 July | 14.15 | 195mph |

### Wendover Airfield

| | | | |
|-----|------|------|-------|
| 23 | 11 August | 12.20 | 59mph |
| 24a | 11 August | 15.45 | |
| 24b | 11 August | 16.07 | 116mph |

### Bonneville

| | | | |
|-----|------|------|-------|
| 25 | 12 August | 16.00 | 159mph |
| 26 | 13 August | 11.17 | 163mph |
| 27 | 14 August | 11.12 | 226mph |

### Wendover Airfield

| | | | |
|-----|------|------|-------|
| 28 | 14 August | 16.15 | – |
| 29 | 14 August | 16.25 | – |
| 30 | 14 August | 16.40 | – |
| 31 | 14 August | 16.50 | – |
| 32 | 14 August | 17.10 | – |
| 33 | 14 August | 17.15 | – |
| 34 | 14 August | 17.25 | 140mph |
| 35 | 14 August | 17.35 | – |
| 36 | 15 August | 08.04 | – |
| 37 | 15 August | 08.08 | – |
| 38 | 15 August | 08.23 | – |
| 39 | 15 August | 08.30 | – |
| 40 | 15 August | 08.50 | – |
| 41 | 15 August | 08.57 | – |

### Bonneville

| | | | |
|-----|------|------|-------|
| 42 | 15 August | 17.10 | 168mph |

### Wendover Airfield

| | | | |
|-----|------|------|-------|
| 43 | 16 August | 11.48 | – |
| 44 | 16 August | 12.06 | – |
| 45 | 16 August | 12.50 | – |
| 46 | 16 August | 15.42 | – |

### Bonneville

| | | | |
|-----|------|------|-------|
| 47 | 17 August | 13.35 | 68mph |
| 48 | 17 August | 16.44 | 313mph |
| 49 | 18 August | 08.38 | 354mph |

**RECORD – 317.021MPH**

### Wendover Airfield

| | | | |
|-----|------|------|-------|
| 50 | 21 August | 11.00 | 120mph |
| 51 | 21 August | 12.00 | 120mph |
| 52 | 21 August | 12.00 | 120mph |
| 53 | 21 August | 12.00 | 120mph |

### Bonneville

| | | | |
|-----|------|------|-------|
| 54a | 22 August | abort | |
| 54 | 22 August | 09.37 | 324mph |
| 55 | 22 August | 10.28 | 342mph |

**RECORD – 328.767MPH**

| | | | |
|-----|------|------|-------|
| 56 | 23 August | 07.35 | 365mph |
| 57 | 23 August | 08.15 | 335mph |

**RECORD – 350.092MPH**

Note: all speeds are peak, VMAX.

# TEAM MEMBERS

## JCB Dieselmax team members

| Name | Team Role | Company | Name | Team Role | Company |
|---|---|---|---|---|---|
| Ron Ayers | Project Aerodynamicist | JCB | Richard King | Performance and Calibration Engineer | Ricardo |
| Nick Bailey | Engine Build Technician | Ricardo | Joe Landon | Catering – Wendover | |
| Matt Beasley | Project Chief Engineer – Engines | Ricardo | Geoff Lattimer | Procurement Engineer – Engines | Ricardo |
| Rod Benoist | Manager – Race Operations | Visioneering | Tim Leverton | Project Director | JCB |
| Annie Berrisford | Team Support & JCB Undergraduate | JCB | Geraint Lewis | Team Support | |
| John Bingham | Vehicle Dynamics | Visioneering | Steve Lewis | Transmission Engineer | JCB |
| Jim Bodle | Truck Driver | JCB | Alistair Macqueen | Race Engineer | Visioneering |
| Colin Bond | JCB Events Project Manager and Push Truck Driver | JCB | Rob Millar | Designer – Electrical System | Visioneering |
| Martin Broadhurst | Mechanic/Car Crew | Visioneering | Dave Minty | Design Engineer – Car | Visioneering |
| David Brown | HI Project Manager | JCB | Davey Nicholas | Technician/Car Crew | Visioneering |
| Paul Brown | Design Engineer – Car | Visioneering | Richard Noble | Project Steering Group Member and Project Mentor | Consultant |
| Michael Charman | Engine Test Technician | Ricardo | Jon Oakey | Chief Designer – Engines | Ricardo |
| Nigel Chell | Press and Communications | JCB | Peter Panarisi | Press and Communications | Fingal |
| Brian Coombes | Design Engineer – Car | Visioneering | Richard Penning | Vehicle Performance Simulation Engineer | Ricardo |
| Richard Cornwell | Lead Performance & Calibration Engineer | Ricardo | Ian Penny | Project Sponsor and Ricardo Global Diesel Director | Ricardo |
| Eoin Corrigan | Fabricator/Car Crew | Visioneering | John Piper | Project Chief Designer – Car | Visioneering |
| Mark Davies | Technician/Car Crew | Visioneering | Brendan Prebo | Press and Communications | JCB |
| Chris Dee | Senior Technician/Car Crew Chief | Visioneering | Graham Richardson | Catering – Wittering | |
| Chris Edwards | Composite Technician/Car Crew | Visioneering | Baptiste Rossi | Body Engineer – Car | Visioneering |
| Simon Evans | Project Steering Group Member and JCB Transmissions Chief Engineer | JCB | Daan Schreuders | Design Engineer – Car | Visioneering |
| | | | Duffy Sheardown | Programme Manager | Visioneering |
| Bryan Ferguson | Operations Director – Visioneering | Visioneering | Neil Smith | Event Management | JCB |
| Teena Gade | Data Acquisition/Electrical Systems Engineer | Visioneering | Taku Takamara | Design Engineer – Car | Visioneering |
| Amanda Gadaselli | Press and Communications | Fingal | Jules Tipler | Press and Communications | Fingal |
| Sophy Gardner | Team Support | RAF | Alan Tolley | Project Steering Group Member and JCB Engine Programmes Director | JCB |
| Andy Green | Driver | RAF | | | |
| Mark Guy | Senior Engine Test Technician | Ricardo | Mike Turner | Industrial Designer – Car Body Surface | JCB |
| Dave Haggas | Car Bodywork Composite Specialist | Visioneering | David Tremayne | Project biographer/consultant | Restless Spirit Racing |
| James Harrington | Ricardo Marketing Manager | Ricardo | Chris Ward | Performance and Calibration Engineer | Ricardo |
| Brian Horner | Chief Executive – Visioneering | Visioneering | Daniel Ward | Project Communications and JCB Worldwide Communications Manager | JCB |
| David Hoyle | Transmissions Manager | JCB | | | |
| Keith Johnson | Truck Driver | JCB | Eric White | Thermal Systems Engineer | Ricardo |
| Ron Jones | Engine Build Technician | Ricardo | Andy Williams | Electronics and Control Systems Manager | JCB |

# INDEX